Affect and Realism in
Contemporary Brazilian Fiction

Affect and Realism in Contemporary Brazilian Fiction

Karl Erik Schøllhammer

Translated from Portuguese by
Marco Alexandre de Oliveira

ANTHEM PRESS

Anthem Press
An imprint of Wimbledon Publishing Company
www.anthempress.com

This edition first published in UK and USA 2022
by ANTHEM PRESS
75–76 Blackfriars Road, London SE1 8HA, UK
or PO Box 9779, London SW19 7ZG, UK
and
244 Madison Ave #116, New York, NY 10016, USA

First published in the UK and USA by Anthem Press in 2020

Copyright © Karl Erik Schøllhammer 2022

The author asserts the moral right to be identified as the author of this work.

All rights reserved. Without limiting the rights under copyright reserved above,
no part of this publication may be reproduced, stored or introduced into
a retrieval system, or transmitted, in any form or by any means
(electronic, mechanical, photocopying, recording or otherwise),
without the prior written permission of both the copyright
owner and the above publisher of this book.

British Library Cataloguing-in-Publication Data
A catalogue record for this book is available from the British Library.

Library of Congress Control Number: 2020946320

ISBN-13: 978-1-83998-540-9 (Pbk)
ISBN-10: 1-83998-540-2 (Pbk)

This title is also available as an e-book.

CONTENTS

Preface	vii
1. The Contemporary in Current Brazilian Literature	1
A Pact with History	8
The Natural History of the Dictatorship	19
2. Realisms in Question	25
From Realism to Post-Realism	28
3. A Paper World—Reflections on the Realism of Luiz Ruffato	35
Everyday Life	44
Notes on Postautonomy	53
4. Brazilian Literature and the Market	61
The Spy, *by Paulo Coelho*	66
Blood-Drenched Beard, *by Daniel Galera*	68
5. The Victorious Return of the Self in Contemporary Writing	71
6. Criticism from the Periphery—for Another Misplaced Idea	87
7. The Challenge of the Sensible and the Sublime Revisited	101
8. Farewell to the Contemporary!	111
Bibliography	119
Index	127

PREFACE

The book is a result of my continuous research performed over the past few years, always discussing a fiction concerned with the possibilities of literary intervention in the reality of the historical moment. Thus, an understanding of the actual role of literature is strategic in the definition of the contemporary, and the book starts with a hypothesis of a certain optimism among current writers and artists with respect to the aesthetic, ethical, and political role of literature and art in the twentieth century. This book pursues a discussion of contemporary Brazilian fiction, mainly the production that has guided the past two decades. It is recognizably difficult, if not impossible, to take account of the full diversity of the prose during this period in Brazil, and the thematic topics raised by each chapter aim to organize our understanding of what characterizes contemporary fiction.

For this reason, as indicated in the title, two axes of reading stand out around a overhauled understanding of realism, on the one hand, and, on the other, of the relevance of affect in the assessment of the role of literary production in current Brazilian literature. With an emphasis on the relation between realism and affect, representation and interpretation are abandoned as a primordial axis of reading and instead an explanation of historical experience in the materiality of aesthetic experience itself is sought. From this perspective, the goal is to show how this reality is manifested on the body of the reader, in the way, for example, the work "touches" its reader like an atmosphere, a sensible climate or attunement or disharmony, leaving the mark of the physical and material encounter that is performed objectively and immediately in reading, and that promotes a concrete historical mediation with its specific context and environment.

Recent literary studies of Brazil generally accept that there was a transformation in the 1960s and 1970s, from a narrative mainly situated in regional areas of the backlands, to the appearance of the big city as a contradictory scenario for national literature. Novelists and short story writers who are consolidated at that time encounter in the big cities of São Paulo and Rio de Janeiro a reality that not only brought a promise of modernity but also produced a civic marginality that came with extreme poverty, violence, and organized crime. In the 1990s and 2000s, a generation of writers appeared who revived programmatic principles of this urban prose and who began the new century with a stronger demand for the real. Such a demand included references from historical realism and at the same time preserved a desire to experiment aesthetically in search of effects and affects, through a performative writing that was articulated in the translation of the historical temporality, mainly in the exploration of a lived presence. The narratives discussed are situated in a spatial referentiality that abandons the imaginary construction of the nation, an important task of modern literature, in favor of stories that are globalized by exploring ways to include Brazilian culture and language in new international networks. In contemporary Brazilian prose, two simultaneous ambitions are often reconciled. The commitment to individual or social reality is a challenge that is assumed without thereby necessarily accepting and following the molds of the traditional search for national or cultural identities. Critics recognize this foundation as one of the constants of modern and contemporary prose, without thereby eliminating the continuous existence of a formal experimentalism that is the clearest heir of the modernist project.

In the first chapter, "The Contemporary in Current Brazilian Literature," current definitions of the contemporary are discussed from the perspective of their understanding of historical time and the importance of lived presence as an often traumatic mediation between personal and historical experience. A certain return to the historical novel becomes evident, not only as a new "pact with history," but also in the discussion of the novel *The Natural History of the Dictatorship*, by working with objectified experiences of recent history in which the narrator abandons biographical intimacy in the exploration of links between biography and its interaction with political events. Chapters 2 and 3, "Realisms in Question" and "A Paper World," address the question of realism in contemporary fiction with regard to the theoretical understanding of historical realism. There is an emphasis on the passage from a literary and artistic project of representational realism to an anti-representational realism that emphasizes the traumatic, the indexical, the affective, in attention to the performance of the real. Among many examples, the third chapter is dedicated to a reading of a few books by the Minas Gerais author Luiz Ruffato, whose work is considered an example of the transformation of the Brazilian novel during the past few decades.

Chapter 4, "Brazilian Literature and the Market," discusses contemporary literature in its optimistic interaction with an expanding and globalized national literary market, and a few examples of writers, such as Paulo Coelho and Daniel Galera, with more popular and commercial approaches to narrative. With the expansion of the market, there was a transformation in the relation of the author's persona with the market and with readers, and there was an exploitation of the actual private figure of the writer in his or her interaction with historical reality, which is termed autofiction. This tendency is debated in Chapter 5, "The Victorious Return of the Self in Contemporary Writing," in comparison with modernist criticisms of lyricism and the figure of the romantic author. With the globalization of the literary market, the very foundation of the nation as a basis and perspective for literature produced in the country becomes a topic of debate. Chapter 6, "Criticism from the Periphery: For Another Misplaced Idea," is thus concerned with exploring, from a perspective of world literature, the different positions in the current critical debate of literary studies in Brazil and how they detach today from a historical hypothesis of global cultural dependency in the formation of national literature.

Chapter 7, "The Challenge of the Sensible and the Sublime Revisited," investigates the question of the sensible from the perspective of twentieth-century critical theory and the postmodern debate around the sublime. Finally, Chapter 8, "Farewell to the Contemporary!" reconsiders this book's initial project under the impression of the cultural turn that has occurred with the present economic and political crisis, now under the neo-populist and authoritarian flag of the current government. From the beginning, the readings have sought to detect the way that contemporary narrative explores its affective potential always in the spatiotemporal concreteness of its fictional construction. It has been shown how the beginning of the century came with a fictional perception of global borders being enhanced and national territories redefined. By a reading of narratives from the present the final chapter ends up discussing how certain narratives today explore the resilience of the past.

Chapter 1

THE CONTEMPORARY IN CURRENT BRAZILIAN LITERATURE*

Time is once more a neuralgic point of reflection when it comes to approaching the fiction written in Brazil today. After the effervescent phase in the debate between the modern and the postmodern, as writers are no longer classified by generation nor are periods or ages firmly characterized, the attempt to understand current literary production has opted for the idea of the "contemporary" in a nonbanal sense of the word. Moving beyond the sense of the simple coincidence between one writer and another, the concept critically introduces an idea that is more committed to the perspective of the simultaneous and to the notion of simultaneity among anachronistic times, thus subverting the conventionally historical continuity of past, present and future. Contrary to this modern historicity, the contemporary points to the simultaneity among historical times as a result of the dilation of a present time that is extensive and constantly open to the past that is intrinsic to it. The fundamental premise of this reformulation is the diagnosis that the present no longer serves as a bridge between the past and the future, but rather emerges as a discontinuous cross-section in a history that no longer guarantees meaning to phenomena. In spite of a present that is full of historical events, the contemporary produces the sensation of being faced with an uncertain and menacing future that has somehow already installed itself, while the past invades the present in the form of memories, images, simulacra and indexes. Thus, the present is paralyzed and becomes bound to the growing presence of a past that does not pass, that we are unable to elaborate, a past that is a living and constantly revitalized image, a type of image that invites one to perform a great rescue project. In this sense, the simultaneity of the contemporary present is the simultaneous presence of a plurality of pasts in an extensive present without clear limits.

One of the effects of this situation is the sensation of a certain historical vacuum, in political and aesthetic terms, for the Brazilian writer. The sense

---

* This was first published in a reduced version as "O contemporâneo na ficção brasileira" in *Humanidades, 44, Brasília,* 2011.

of resistance to the authoritarian regime, which guided a significant part of the production of the 1970s and 1980s, has been lost, along with any possible enthusiasm for the democratization of the 1990s, which was nourished by the fall of the Berlin Wall, and also by the geopolitical direction that guided art and literature in dialogue with cultural and postcolonial studies at the end of the twentieth century. Obviously, there is no lack of political and social causes in Brazil today, but it is necessary to understand how art in general, and literature in particular, will be able to regain relevance within this context. In a world where reading represents a minimal part of cultural reception, it is understandable that literature loses relevance. It is graver, however, to recognize that literature has shown itself incapable of accompanying and coordinating responses to the growing complexity of this reality, even becoming aware of this loss of impact on the whole of contemporary artistic and cultural production. Traditionally a generator of new forms of imagination and a creator of narrative relations among all dimensions of reality, literature has diminished in the face of the industrial capacity of the media to create or suggest possible worlds. The sensation that we as readers are living through a moment ruled by the recycling of literary projects of the past reflects the disorientation in the search for a response to this situation, in which literature no longer counts on the creative autonomy that in modernity was understood as a historical role. Publishers seem to be aware of the problem and look to create stimulating and exotic settings for literary production, such as, for example, the Amores Expressos (Love Express) project, whose motto, curiously enough, seems more like an old-school doctor's advice to improve the creative health of an anemic patient: "Travel to distant lands and create a love story!" The challenge in the face of this flattening tendency in literature should be, on the contrary, to try to reflect on that which only literary writing is capable of being or doing, thus reinforcing the need for its existence, which has been called into question.

 Another effect of this diagnosis seems to be the search for presentification, which is always understood in two senses: reclaiming the temporality of the immediate and creating effects of sensible presence. The former is observed by critics in terms of the immediacy of the creative process itself, and the latter can be seen in the anxiety of coordinating and intervening in a troubled present reality. It has been noted that the distance between writing and reading has become shorter, that the interval between creation and reception has diminished technologically, and that the writer who practically writes online experiences the temporality of the media by accentuating the performative aspect of his or her work. Of course, the book continues to be the main vehicle of contemporary literature, but the writer knows that, to make the circulation of merchandise easier, it is important to interact with all the stages of book production, distribution and consumption, which unfold through the media, and it is necessary for the figure of the author to appear in spaces—bookstores, fairs, biennials, launches and so on—in which the public may be attracted by the product or by the literary environment. Authors must become celebrities to some extent, which most achieve by writing short stories in magazines, creating blogs and participating in newspaper columns. In addition, writers give interviews and appear in public, leading lectures, roundtables and mini-courses in direct contact with their potential consumers. On the one hand, the beginning writer looks for shortcuts to literary success by publicizing not always fully developed results in virtual formats or independent publications. On the other, if there is the slightest suspicion by the media establishment that the writer is endowed with any interesting talent, which may then become a product, he or she immediately falls into the personality cult that today is already part of this logic of constant renovation in the literature market. This immediacy offers another creative possibility for the author, who now, more than ever, tells the story of the making of his or her own creations, publicly reflecting on creative processes and on the network of contingencies of the everyday life with which he or she interacts. Thus, a "self-writing" is authorized about the staging of its own creation and production, or of an ethnographic writing that transcribes the constellation of information in which it is included and in which fiction forms a part of a reality that is thereby justified by its erasing of the distinction between reality and fiction. This erasure creates what the Argentinian critic Josefina Ludmer has called "realityfiction" (Ludmer 2010a, 75),[1] whereby fiction gains reality while reality in fiction shifts its status by no longer being only a "historical reality." Instead, it is converted into pure present and pure "everyday reality," as Ludmer observes with respect to Latin American literature. For her, the role that literature assumes today is precisely that of a "reality factory" in the age of the language industry, and it can be added that, in a situation in which dreams, fantasy and the imagination are expropriated by the media, fiction encounters a challenge in exploring the conversion of certain images into reality, thus accentuating its performative and affective dimension.

Nonetheless, today there are also writers who believe in the direct reformulation of social commitment and insist on a fiction that is often the heir of realism, which may have the power to intervene in reality. Such writers intend to create testimonies and write in order to interpret and reflect upon the contemporary history of Brazil and the world, occupying themselves with themes that concern a significant part of society in formats that are often echoed in

---

[1] "realidadficción" in Spanish.

the media and in the public sphere. This anxiety of presence may be seen as a symptom of the revival of the realist project and of the wish to establish a new alliance between literature and society as well as its problems. Such an ambition explains a series of phenomena that we can understand in light of a realist project that does not, however, necessarily accept the narrow representational premises of the historical realisms. The use of brief and hybrid forms, the adaptation of a short and fragmentary language and the flirting with journalistic prose clearly appear in writers such as Fernando Bonassi, Marcelino Freire and Luiz Ruffato, among others. The production by these writers gives an idea of this contemporary urgency, of the desire to speak about and with the real as a way of achieving an effect of critical presence that supposes the revival of historical projects aimed at social commitment and intervention. For these writers, the effects of "presence" are coupled with the conjunction of historical contents in an urban narrative tradition that originated in the 1970s generation of short story writers, and an aesthetic efficiency sought in a more emphatic language and style. For others, the fictional path revives a certain memorialism in the pursuit of private and familiar memories or through a staging of the minutiae of personal life.

From this perspective, presence becomes synonymous with intimacy and literary approximation to the most everyday, autobiographical and banal, the material stuff of ordinary life in its slightest details. Between these two sides there seems to be a constant polarization, which has even been exploited by the media, mostly by the press, as a way of presenting contemporary production through the contrast between two literary aesthetics. On the one hand, there would be the brutality of urban and marginal realism, which assumes its contemporary detachment; on the other, the grace of private and sensible universes that believe in the search for epiphany and the simple story inspired by the everyday lives of everyone. In both most recent narrative tendencies, the insistence on the temporal present expresses, however, the intuition of a difficulty or impossibility, something that keeps fiction from recovering its association with the moment and that is found in the challenge of the immediate, not only in the creation but also in the publication of the work, the contact with the reader and the impact on the public sphere.

The sensation of this impossibility may be further discussed in light of the reading that the Italian philosopher Giorgio Agamben does of the topic in dealing with the question "What is the contemporary?" in a 2006 lecture. Agamben (2009) recovers the observation by Roland Barthes on *Untimely Meditations*, by Nietzsche, as he approximates the concepts of the contemporary and the untimely. The "contemporary is the untimely," Barthes says, which according to Agamben means that the true contemporary is not he who identifies with his time or who is fully in tune with it. On the contrary, the contemporary is he who, due to a difference, a lag or an anachronism, is able to capture his time and to see it. In this sense, contemporary literature will not be that which represents the current moment, unless it does so by an inadequacy, a historical estrangement that makes it perceive the marginal and obscure zones of the present that escape its logic. To be contemporary, according to this line of reasoning, is to be able to find one's way in the dark, and to thereby have the courage to recognize and commit to a present with which it is not possible to coincide.

In current literature, there are clear signs of this urgency of relating to historical reality even without trusting history as an explanation and reason for events. One of the most remarkable features of contemporary art has been, in this paradoxical sense, its "historicism" without a philosophy of history, that is, its inscription in the circumstances in which it is produced at "the same time" that it is not seen as part of this history. In Agamben's writings, this anachronism, this fracture between time and history that characterizes the contemporary, deepens the dilemma of modern man already discussed at length by him in the book *Infancy and History*, from 1978 (1993). The dilemma of contemporary man is that, without an experience of time that is adequate to the experience of history, he finds himself "painfully split between his being-in-time as an elusive flow of instants and his being-in-history, understood as the original dimension of man" (Agamben 1993, 100). Based on this diagnosis, and inspired by Benjamin and Heidegger, Agamben seeks another notion of time, and the concept that he formulates is *kairos*, a time with an existential meaning that is defined in contrast to *kronos*, the anonymous flow of continuous time. In *kairos*, man experiences "the abrupt and sudden conjunction where decision grasps opportunity and life is fulfilled in the moment" (101). One perceives that Agamben speaks here of an existential dimension of time, a temporal experience in which man sees and seizes his historical opportunity, his freedom and his happiness by freeing the moment from the empty continuity of pseudo-historicism in favor of the kairological time of authentic history. If this idea of the qualitative time of *kairos* is still upheld in the modern ideology of a possible emancipation and future, the later perspective of Agamben will identify this time with the "time that remains," a messianic time inspired by Paul's term for the messianic event: *ho nyn kairos*—"the time of the now." Messianic time is neither the time to come nor the end of time, but rather a "time that contracts itself and begins to end […] the time that remains between time and its end" (Agamben 2005, 62). The philosophical discussion of these terms and the validity of this messianic hope is not relevant to this context, but one can safely say that the perspective here aims at the past, unlike the existential perspective of *Infancy and History*, in which the future was within reach. And it is precisely the growing presence of the past that characterizes the dilated time of the contemporary, an anachronism described by Agamben that may help us to understand the focus on the past, on memory and on history, however, always from the perspective of their presence, from the way they are made present in everyday life. Josefina Ludmer describes the way to narrate the past as follows:

> Now the past is set in the present, and temporality takes the form of a series of blocks, with interruptions, fractures, and repetitions. They are narrative fragments, it is a way of organizing the narration through fragments that flow in a sort of series. A series that can go on indefinitely, a series that is not unified or totalized. This temporality is the time of the now, and for some, it is also the pure present of reality. It is also the temporality and the narrative form of the media and melodrama: a pure present, dense with images of different speeds that expropriates all pasts in the form of nostalgia, memory, or pain. (Ludmer 2010a, 77)[2]

In addition to circumscribing the complicity between the ways that contemporary fiction tends to narrate the past and the melodramatic narratives of the media and commercial cinema, one may guess that a view of history is expressed which does not only celebrate and revise the past in nostalgic and melancholic terms, as occurred in the modernist reformulation of the grand national narratives of the twentieth century and even in the metahistorical (postmodern) novels of the 1980s. In the contemporary, the identitarian link with history has been broken, and the narratives seek to restore this lost perspective based on a supposedly (hypothetically?) irreparable disaster. Time is no longer driven toward the future or toward an end to be realized by progress or by subjective emancipation; time now turns to the catastrophe that has interrupted the past. Benjaminian melancholy has become aggravated, and the meaning and truth of the present now seem to be deposited in an experience that is out of reach, a kind of generalized trauma that is converted into a sudden object of desire. Both in the entertainment industry and in literary

---

[2] The original in Spanish reads: "Ahora el pasado está puesto en el presente, y la temporalidad toma la forma de una serie de bloques, con interrupciones, fracturas y repeticiones. Son fragmentos narrativos, es un modo de organizar la narración por fragmentos que se suceden en una especie de serie. Una serie que puede seguir indefinidamente, una serie que no se unifica ni se totaliza. Esa temporalidad es el tiempo del ahora y para algunos es puro presente de la realidad. También es la temporalidad y la forma narrativa de los medios y del melodrama: un presente puro, denso, de imágenes de diferentes velocidades que expropia todos los pasados en forma de nostalgia, memoria o duelo." Unless otherwise indicated, all translations from the Portuguese and Spanish are by Marco Alexandre de Oliveira.

and cinematic fiction, one observes a true "traumatophilia" that has become the preferred heuristic way of narrating the past, a search for the inaugural disaster (of which everyone in some manner is a part) that is no longer the limit of all experience and identity, but rather their point of departure and condition of possibility.

From Bernardo Carvalho, Milton Hatoum, João Gilberto Noll and Cristóvão Tezza to the more recent Cecília Giannetti, João Anzanello Carrascoza and Michel Laub, narratives built upon the figure of trauma have become the preferred psychoanalytic fiction. They allow the personal traumatic incident to metonymically refer to the trauma of history and thus justify the need to rebuild individual identity into a broader, historical identity, which the writer attempts to recover. The search for the past in collective or biographical memory is intensified on account of a passion for the real that no longer distinguishes what in fact has occurred from that which the imagination has symptomatically created. From the perspective of trauma, the real and phantasmatic effects are the same, and one notes that a good part of current artistic production, particularly that driven by the emphatic interest in the (auto)biographical, may be understood in tune with testimony as the staging of a self-victimization that yearns to give some meaning to existence, and in relation to which confessional intimacy acquires a new authority. The notion of "traumatophilia" serves, therefore, to help one understand the intrinsic affinity between, on the one hand, a literary style that explores the shock effects of this radical reality, with references to an aesthetics of transgression and of the abject, and, on the other, a tendency that is opposed to it, that is opposed to the aesthetics of cruelty and that reclaims the everyday, the intimate, the private and the common as sources of an experience anchored in a time that is more vivid and real. Thus, the plunge into everyday and intimate processes, which involve basic affects such as pain, fear, melancholy and desire, appears once again in contemporary fiction, but without the stigma of the psychological or intimist tendency of the 1950s and 1960s. Now, such a tendency is legitimized via the exploration of personal experiences endured in the flesh, of their techniques of presence and creative affirmation of private devices in an inhuman, massifying and alienating culture. Trauma offers a meaning, on the one hand, for the extremes of exceptional experiences, always close to the objects explored by the sensationalist media, and, on the other, for the return to the private universe in which traditional confessionalism resuscitates with a new legitimacy in the exploration of the (auto)biographical differential that defines the individual to the extent that it makes him or her a victim of his or her particular condition.

The fusion of the two perspectives typically coincides with the inversion between public spaces and private spheres that occurs when the figure of the artist or the writer appears in the media, thus relegating the work to a secondary level that is always in the shadow of his or her private and biographical life. It is now the case that private products—diaries, letters or autobiographical accounts—have become more interesting than the actual works, even by highly recognized artists and writers. In a way, trauma has become chic, has turned into a cover story for culture magazines, and its enormous visibility in the current media expresses a banalization of suffering in a generalized celebrity culture. This overexposure of biographical experiences, which is confused with the general media strategy, indicates the contemporary promiscuity between the psychic and the social—between the outside, the world, and the inside, the subject—in a pathologized public sphere in which individual suffering is experienced as collective and intimacy is only achieved through public exposure. Unfortunately, a part of contemporary literature corroborates this tendency and explores its public attraction—in an attempt to gain credibility, legitimacy and attention—to the extent that it really or fictionally takes private life as the creative material of choice.

A Pact with History[†]

One of the main challenges for contemporary Brazilian writers has become to write about our time, to bring historical references inside the narrative and thus gain reality in the present. Some authors return to traditional historical topics in the attempt to make an implicit knowledge emerge, which the narrative may unfold little by little. Thus, contemporary literature still lives under the spell of the question of realism, of how literature relates to reality, whether as a reference of its expression or as a target of its gesture. Writers care about the world, become responsible for the place in which they live and seek to intervene in a significant way. Politically, ethically, and aesthetically, literature may be regarded as an instrument for transformation. Therefore, realism is still a program assumed by some contemporaries in its historical sense, as a question of representation, similar to what was proposed by nineteenth-century writers. For others, the commitment is closer to the various new realisms that arose throughout the twentieth century. Here, representation gives way to an idea of performative intervention by means of poetic effects awakened in different experiments to express this same historical reality, which is now freed from the illusions of fidelity and representational veracity. Twentieth-century Brazilian literature remained faithful to the ideal of historical realism via regionalism

---

[†] A previous version was published as "O pacto renovado com a história—o realismo contemporâneo brasileiro" in *Ciência Hoje*, 288.

and urban fiction. In the twenty-first century, this pact has been renewed by various writers who have been defining the direction of contemporary literature. Nonetheless, one observes a contradiction between the literary project that originated in the beginning of modernity, which was tied to confidence in the enlightening powers of representation over the mind of the reader, and the search for a new performative potency of writing, which can recover the historical role of literature in a predominantly visual and media culture. We live in a moment that makes it difficult to distinguish clearly among fictionists. This lack of a definition of the contemporary has often been confused with creative diversity and with a certain permissive liberalism that would justify the revival of literary and aesthetic-political questions without a concern for their contexts of origin. Innovation and tradition thus crisscross, but rarely generate a serious and daring reformulation of the problems invoked by the narrative experiments put into practice by the authors.

Two novels offer samples of what may be understood as a reformulated pact with historical realism: *Nowhere People*, by Paulo Scott (2011), and *Desde que o samba é samba* (Ever since samba was samba), by Paulo Lins (2012). The former revives the format of the generational novel, and the latter, that of the historical novel. Both authors represent, each in his own way, literature at the end of the twentieth century. Paulo Lins is the author of *City of God* (1997b), perhaps the most important novel of the 1990s, while Paulo Scott, identified with Generation X and with the Rio Grande do Sul writers Daniel Galera, Joca Reiners Terron, and Daniel Pellizari, gained visibility with the publisher Livros do Mal,[3] and then followed an independent career at large publishing houses.

In a way, Paulo Lins's second novel was a surprise, after an interval of 15 years without publishing fiction. Lins was no longer an author frozen by his own success and suspected of writer's block. Published in 1997 by Companhia das Letras, the most prestigious publisher at that time, and approved by renowned intellectuals such as Roberto Schwarz, Lins's debut novel attracted tremendous critical attention. The rapid success of the film version by Fernando Meirelles overshadowed the discussion on the actual novel, which was absorbed by the adaptation to the point of opting for shorter versions to make them closer to the film's narrative. From this perspective, it

---

[3] Paulo Scott debuted in 2001 with the book of short stories *Histórias curtas para domesticar as paixões dos anjos e atenuar o sofrimento dos monstros* [Short stories to domesticate the passions of angels and ease the suffering of monsters], but it was with *Ainda orangotangos* [Still orangatangs, 2003] and then with the novel *Voláteis* [Volatile, 2005] that he sparked more attention.

is important to read the novel *Desde que o samba é samba* (2012), situated in the historical setting of Rio de Janeiro in the 1920s and built around not only emblematic samba figures, such as Ismael Silva, Alcebíades Barcelos, Heitor dos Prazeres and the singer Francisco Alves, but also some modernist writers, such as Mário de Andrade and Manuel Bandeira. The story refers to peripheral places where *malandroism* and other types of marginality reigned, such as the Mangue (Marsh) prostitution district, São Carlos Hill, and the Estácio neighborhood, which was the birthplace of the first samba school of Brazil, Deixa Falar (Let them speak), founded in 1928. The reader is introduced to picturesque places such as the Bar Apolo, the Café do Compadre, and the house of the Bahian woman Hilária Batista de Almeida, better known as Tia Ciata, where the *sambistas* at the time gathered. Employing episodes of violence and police repression, the plot seeks to make evident the straight ties among samba, *malandroism*, capoeira, and Umbanda centers.[4] The main character is Sílvio Fernandes, or "Brancura" (Whiteness), a *sambista* from Estácio and also a pimp, *malandro*, and *capoeirista* fighter, a great lover inserted in a fictional love triangle with the prostitute Valdirene and the Portuguese man Sodré, an employee of the Banco do Brasil (Bank of Brazil) who ends up becoming a pimp and marijuana dealer. The novel additionally provokes discussion between historians and critics as a result of certain polemical affirmations, such as the homosexuality of Ismael Silva and the sinuous relations between samba and the beginning of organized crime.

City of God roused attention due to the mixture of historical-sociological research and the author's own "testimony" of the narrated events, which occurred over the course of three decades in a Rio de Janeiro neighborhood whose decadence shaped a very faithful image of the recent history of the city. These "strong" references to reality in the exemplary and almost allegorical narrative created a powerful formula in which the *brutalist* urban prose of the 1960s and 1970s was combined with the "classical" format of the historical novel, also incorporating some expressive characteristics of modernism. The lack of complexity and personal life of the characters is compensated by the capacity to show the decomposition of the social and cultural structures in tune with the violence and marginal exclusion. On this point, the fiction attributed a different meaning to the events narrated, which surpassed the mere interest in the storyline. In Lins's new novel, historical research is also the backdrop of the intrigue, at times being superimposed on the internal logic of the story, and the way that samba is described in its origins, at the margin of society and imbedded in a marginal culture of delinquency and repression,

---

[4] Translator's note: Umbanda refers to a syncretic, Afro-Brazilian spiritual tradition.

offers an allegorical perspective to the work, much like the writing of Jorge Amado, who always knew how to manage the erotic density of his characters, which for its part is culturally exemplary. Lins goes down the path of desire as well, his main characters guided by an unrestrainable libido that, unfortunately, falls into a tedious writing of mechanically narrated sex scenes, which is unable to achieve either the smooth seduction of Amado or the priapic satire of Reinaldo Morais.

In the 1980s, one of the characteristics of the so-called postmodern movement was the recycling of the historical novel via the anachronistic metanarrative in which rereadings of the past—such as *Viva o povo brasileiro* (Long live the Brazilian people), by João Ubaldo Ribeiro, *Boca do inferno* (Hell's mouth), by Ana Miranda, and *Agosto* (August), by Rubem Fonseca—revised history from the perspective of the Brazilian present. This postmodern permissiveness in the recycling of the grand narratives of the past freed the will to fable from the hermetic snares of modernism, and the appreciation of good stories was maintained among contemporaries. Traditional formats of the great modern novel—the regional novel, coming-of-age novel, memoir novel, travel novel and so on—reappeared in the new millennium with renewed vigor among writers such as Luiz Ruffato (*Inferno provisório*, or "Temporary hell"), Silviano Santiago (*Heranças*, or "Inheritances"), Chico Buarque de Holanda (*Leite derramado*, or "Spilt milk") and Marçal Aquino (*Eu receberia as piores notícias de seus lindos lábios*, or "I'd receive the worst news from your beautiful lips"), and the ties to historical realism were reconfirmed, whether updated or not by the desire to create real effects and affects through the experiment of literary creation beyond the mere commitment to representation. Some authors were more successful than others, but, in any case, the revival of realist experiments raises a fundamental challenge for writers: to make evident the fictional potency of literature in a cultural reality stunned by the media production of reality, taking into account that the anxiety for documentary recovery occupies a large part of a market flooded with memoirs, biographies, popular history books, testimonies, statements, interviews, reports, confessions, news stories and other variations of nonfiction. Faced with the daily tsunami of realism that threatens to drown the reader, what type of reality can literature offer?

In *Nowhere People*, his most ambitious novel, the Rio Grande do Sul writer Paulo Scott bravely faces the task of narrating facts that marked the last generation of the twentieth century. In the plot, the character Paulo, a 21-year-old militant in the student movement, a law intern and rising star in the Workers' Party who is one step away from taking power, decides to take a break and review his priorities. He meets a 14-year-old Guarani indigenous girl on the side of the highway and experiences a strange and unexplainable attraction to her, with whom he begins an impossible relationship that ends in a disastrous confusion with the police and forces him to travel to London, abandoning the pregnant girl to the mercy of her deplorable fate. With the firm hand of an artisan, Scott narrates the story in an epic rhythm with a growing complexity and the clear ambition to reconcile the circumstantial data of the story, in light of national myths such as that of Iracema, by evoking the discrete hope of a contemporary Brazil at peace with its past demons.

Although literary and ethical ambitions evidently drive the novel, the problem is that the understanding of recent Brazilian history does not seem sufficiently leveraged by the narrative: the characters depend on an omniscient narrator who always emerges to explain to the readers what they, the characters, really think and feel. In his theory of the novel, Milan Kundera (2003) insists that the narrator should never be more intelligent than the characters—and much less the author. In order to come to life, the narrative has to be guided by the intrinsic logic of actions, and not by the didactic or moral intentions of its creator. The narrator should let go of this role so that the fiction may offer an understanding of the material narrated that escapes even the author. That is what distinguishes, according to Kundera, literary fiction from the "general fiction," which is predominant in all areas of story consumption—in the media, in telenovelas, in the fiction of any of the entertainment genres and in commercial cinema. The understanding of history, even in its traditional formats, always depends on narrative techniques, and, as is well known, fictional devices are also recognized in scientific discourses. However, if fiction and the narrative exist both in scientific history and in the novel, literature must then show what it and only it can do and what no other media, no other discourse can: create a constellation of events, causality, coincidences and other factors, concrete or imaginary, such as, for example, the overlapping relations among music, religion and crime in Lins's novel, or the link between democracy and disappointment in the post-Berlin Wall geopolitics of Brazil, in the case of Scott. The movement is retrospective, and what brings this landscape into perspective is the present, a present that does not guarantee, however, the evolutionary continuity of history, but rather thematizes a rupture by which not only the past but also the future is modified. The setting of an easily recognizable history is offered for the development of a fictional plot that includes private and autofictional intimacy to thematize the official narrative of democratization. It is the transition process interrupted by the confusion of political indigestions, it is the end of hope that initiates a sort of posthistorical time in which the ghost of history returns to the present naturalized in the myth of Iracema.

This does not concern interpreting and analyzing history, but of making it possible for it to touch us in its immanent sense and involve us affectively. When contemporary writers approach history, by reformulating their commitment to the real world, their raw material is the more or less historicized imagination, while their narrative and fictional tools are no different than those of the historian or journalist. The reality of the text does not depend on its references or on its representational faithfulness. It arises in the voice that touches us without mediation or justification, it emerges from the personal life of the characters and from the ethical and political desire to listen to and be moved by the events staged.

In other examples of novels, we could identify the followers of the metahistorical narrative, repeatedly highlighted in the context of so-called postmodern experiments, in which fiction rethinks historiography and even the notion of time and its modern assumptions of continuity and synchrony. For instance, there is the novel *The Mystery of Rio*, by Alberto Mussa, whose detective story is situated in the *belle époque* of Rio de Janeiro and unfolds in nonlinear fashion through anachronistic temporal spirals that encompass even precolonial history. Without going into further details with regard to the cited examples, it is enough to say that they indicate a recent literary historicism that would be interesting to discuss from the broader perspective of its epistemological strategies for giving reality to the present, to the contemporary experience.

A fundamental condition for this view is to recognize what Hans Ulrich Gumbrecht called the *broad present* as a phenomenological condition of the contemporary. As is well known, the temporality of the present was already crucial for the modernist search for an instant pregnant with novelty and innovation, and the demand for presentification aimed to wrest the embryonic future from the full present recreated in the gesture of modernist art and literature. For writers and artists at the beginning of the twenty-first century, however, the present is only experienced as a failed encounter with history, a "not yet" or an "already," as formulated by Lyotard (1991a), for whom the postmodern sublime meant an existential positioning in the face of this impossibility. In the "nowness" of the aesthetic present, Lyotard saw a potency that, instead of opening itself up as the modern utopian promise of something better on the historical horizon, is presentified in affective experience as a pure possibility of change in the relation between the subject and its reality, and simultaneously, as a threat that nothing will happen. If the modernist present offered a way to realize a qualitative time that communicated with history in a redemptive manner, the contemporary present breaks the backbone of history and offers neither rest nor reconciliation. The past is only presentified as lost, offering the testimony of its disconnected indexes, which become raw material for the archival impulse. Meanwhile, the future only becomes meaningful through an untimely action capable of dealing with the anachronisms.

In the award-winning novel by Michel Laub, *Diary of the Fall* (2014), there is an example of how the development of the protagonist is mirrored in the trauma of the grandfather, a survivor of the concentration camps. The account of how the narrator participates in a violent episode of bullying at a Jewish school in Porto Alegre against his friend João, a poor non-Jewish boy who almost died in the incident, adds authenticity to the narrative due to its inverted parallelism with the Holocaust, which was experienced and silenced by the protagonist's grandfather. This authenticity is exacerbated by the suggestive way in which the novel indicates that it is about a true story of the writer's family. All the biographical affinities built in the narrative point in this direction. Like the author, Michel Laub, the protagonist is an almost 40-year-old Rio Grande do Sul writer and narrates the story in the present. Nevertheless, the novel's release explains: "Not one of Laub's grandfathers was a prisoner, but he has a cousin whose grandfather was sent to a concentration camp." That is, the story is not really autobiographical, and even so it still is, for the reflection and the gravity of the historical trauma affect everyone and become the final reference for any intention of touching the real. In the novel *A Poison Apple* (2013), the second volume of Laub's disaster trilogy, the stories of Kurt Cobain's suicide and the heroic survival of the writer Immaculée Ilibagiza at the massacre during the Rwanda war echo in the death of Valéria, the narrator's girlfriend, who is once more an autofictional figure that is confused with the author. The boundaries between reality and fiction are erased, and under the impact of trauma a personal history becomes identified with the tragic events of the twentieth century. However, it concerns an unauthorized appropriation that, despite perhaps being driven by a sincere interest and genuine empathy with the victims of real violence, ends up exploiting in the name of good intentions the pain and suffering of the victims, who are silenced by history.

By plunging into the inexpressible of the small pain, one builds a metonymic relation to pain in its maximum and unimaginable reality, which suggests a kind of perverse community authorizing the small voice in the absence of the large one. According to Mark Seltzer (1995), we are living under the impact of a "wound culture," which becomes evident in a kind of inversion of the public sphere, in which intimacy is exposed as the interior of an inside-out coat that is exhibited and experienced in public in a constant short-circuit between the individual and the multitude. It concerns a spectacular voyeurism that is nourished by the fascination for the exposure of large and small atrocities, a pathologization of the public sphere that is emphatically shared around traumatic wounds, a suffering that somehow becomes collective, for it emotionally unites and involves everyone at a time when brutalization and indifference seem to affect the private sphere and private experience. The consequences are notable and produce an ambiguity that threatens the solid boundaries between collective forms of representation, exposure and testimony and the singularity or privacy of the subject. The generalization of trauma is expressed in the confusion between the psychic and the social, between the outside, the world, and the inside, the subject. It creates a public sphere around a pathetic passion that allows for the sharing of suffering as an affective link of collectivity, while intimacy is reshaped according to media exposure.

The impact of this culture of trauma differs from that of the modern culture of shock, as analyzed by Baudelaire via Benjamin in the twentieth century. If shock was an outside impact on the subject determined by the drastic transformations of modernity, the culture of trauma is a culture that interiorizes impact, a culture in which it is difficult to discern the outside and the inside, perception and fantasy, the physical and the psychic, and even cause and effect. This doubt is instilled and motivated by the particular temporality of trauma, which Freud called *nachträglich* in characterizing an experience so shocking that it is blocked by the psychic apparatus and only reflected a posteriori by the symptoms deferred from their original reality. *Nachträglichkeit* has been translated as "afterwardsness" or "deferred action," terms that do not effectively handle the idea of an event of rupture in the past that spreads to the present in a symptomatic expression that is always incomplete and indicative of something that happened and which is forever lost, unless it is recovered through a process of approximation and recognition in analysis. Seltzer associates himself with the more radical diagnoses of contemporary reality, dialoguing with theorists such as Hal Foster and Slavoj Žižek, for whom the exploration of violence and shock, both in the media and in art, is understood as a search for a "real," defined as impossible or lost, which cannot be experienced except as a reflection of the limit of one's own experience, as the other side of culture, or as that which is only perceived in the fissures of representation and the threats to symbolic stability.

Taking into consideration this contemporary passion for disaster, it is not by chance that the notion of testimony was asserted in the theoretical field during the 1990s, not only to generate a new understanding of the ever sparse and painful statements on the Holocaust, but also as a heuristic figure of something that we may call an impossible experience, of that which happens at the polar extremes between history and humankind, between violence and the body, between destruction and survival, that which encounters its epistemic figure in the psychoanalytical analysis of trauma. The testimony of the unsayable is the mark left in the discourse of that which was the essence of the real, the defeat of experience and of subjectivity itself, and which will be reproduced and repeated obsessively until succumbing to its own silence. Here we once again identify the already widely analyzed figure of traumatic realism; it is worth recovering its historical origin and pointing out an unfolding that may offer an alternative route of expression. It is good to recall that the aesthetics of trauma nourished itself with a *plus quam perfectae* temporality, the past of the discourse of the past, indicating a sort of lost and postcatastrophic historicity that is only recoverable negatively, through the traces and clues of the impossibility of its articulation. In the bibliography about the figure of trauma as a heuristic prism for a radical understanding of modernity as disaster, the origin is situated in the value given to Eichmann's testimony in the postwar trials, a value that differs from that given by the legal strategy of the Nuremberg trials, which were supported by documentary evidence and files from the Third Reich that fell into the hands of the Allies. During the Eichmann trial in Jerusalem, the survivors of the concentration camps were invited, whose dramatic and emotional testimonies collaborated in the conversion of the trial into a kind of political and historical pedagogy in which not only the evidence was at play, but also the emotions awakened and experienced by the participants.

In an intriguing little book written by both the Israeli architect Eyal Weizman and the American literary critic Thomas Keenan, the two authors suggest the emergence of a third moment in this memory, a moment related to the process of identifying Josef Mengele's bones, which were found in the city of Embu das Artes, in the state of São Paulo, in 1985. The investigation around Mengele's escape to South America generated the hypothesis that the criminal would have spent the last years of his life in São Paulo under a false alias until he drowned in 1979. When, six years later, his grave was opened, an investigative process began that, according to Keenan and Weizman (2012), would inaugurate what they call a forensic aesthetics or forensic paradigm that is markedly different from the aforementioned documentary paradigm of the Nuremberg trials and testimonial paradigm of the Eichmann trial in Jerusalem, at the beginning of the 1960s. The challenge for the legal team was to identify with scientific certainty (i.e., even beyond circumstantial probability) that the bones found in Embu das Artes were those of Josef Mengele. This was the spark for a series of investigations, which occurred in 1985, of mortal remains belonging to the "disappeared" of the Argentinian dictatorship. After the finding of Mengele's bones, several scientists were called to participate as experts in trials on crimes against human rights and invited to speak and interpret the objects that constituted evidence, often bones and human remains. Thus began a practice of investigation based on new forensic technology and an expository rhetoric of the signification of these objective remains that as a whole characterize the forensic paradigm, which extrapolates in many ways the field of law. It concerns an epistemological change that quickly comes to influence legal practices as a new cultural sensibility, an ethics and a political aesthetics whose implications and influences quickly overflowed the boundaries of their initial forums and made their way from the juridical field to structure the way we understand and represent political conflicts, whether in media, in political debates, in literature, film, or the arts. (Keenan and Weizman 2012, 13–14)

In the scope of forensic investigation, normally the aim is to determine what exactly occurred at the scene of the crime, but in the case of Mengele's bones, the question was, who are you? It concerned identifying the mortal remains from a biographical perspective, seeking the marks of events, accidents, violence, and diseases recorded in the person's body. Thus, the bones were no longer considered a part of a human life nor only an object; they were read as printed marks of a lived life, like a surface maculated by its exposure to life, just as a photograph results from its exposure to light. Clyde Snow, the coroner for the case, baptized the work of identifying the human remains as bone biography, or *osteobiography*. With the use of new video technology, the team elaborated an exhibition of superimposed images of Mengele's life with photos of his skull, all of which was able to convince the judges of the perfect coincidence between the object (the skull) and the person (Mengele's face).

The trial involving Mengele's identity was the fundamental beginning of the identification of disappeared people, and it coincidentally inaugurated a technology that was crucial in Latin American human rights trials by making it possible to restore the biographies and histories of thousands of anonymous bodies hidden in dictatorship graveyards. In the following decades, these novelties were applied in various countries, and the common grave began to occupy the central place—from the perspective of testimony—that the concentration camp had occupied as the *Nomos* of modernity according to Giorgio Agamben. At the same time, the case of Mengele's bones indicated a shift in perspective in contemporary culture, which is more and more fascinated by the tension between the testimonial perspective and the forensic perspective. This tension demands an inclusion of testimony in the political exposition and explanation of reality to a forum for whom the truth becomes visible in its inner narrative cohesion, which is the potential dimension of the forensic. Without the testimonial dimension, the forensic is easily converted into a positivistic belief in the scientific objectivity of facts, and without the forensic dimension, testimony can become an individual expression of the symptomatic consequences of the exposure to the threat of extermination. Only the balanced tension between the two discourses can defend the collective dimension, in which aesthetics regains its political nature and becomes a concrete intervention in the circumstances of real events.

In a large part of contemporary literary production, a double perspective is introduced between the testimony of the threat of individual annihilation and the search for the material remains of historical experience. It is between these extremes that we can situate the novel *Dentes negros* (Black teeth, 2011), by André de Leones, in which history is narrated through a posthistorical science-fiction story that unfolds in a time supposedly after a great calamity in Brazil, a time ambiguously situated between the past and the future. In the universe of youth culture, there are static tendencies characterized as retrofuturist, in which the anxiety for a utopian future is confused with a dream of a distant past. This same ambiguity is evident in Leones's story: it is in the Brazilian countryside, in the state of Goiás, which is already disappearing as a consequence of a great evil that at all times occupies the center of the narrative as if it indicated the true story, the event that changes everything. One reader or another will remember the disaster with Cesium 137 in Goiânia in 1987, the worst nuclear accident that ever occurred in Brazil. Having left four victims, it was a modest tragedy if compared to the real perspective of nuclear destruction. Nonetheless, the novel does not deal with this question: it concerns much more than an exploration of the narrative possibilities "after history," after the great event. In the story told, one perceives the annulment of the subjective part of the characters: Hugo and Renata are survivors whose paths accidentally cross and who have no other project besides survival. There is the soldier Alexandre, stationed in a fort with the mission of reestablishing some order against the anarchy and criminality of the survivors, and there are still other characters, such as the children of "The Twenty-Three" group, threatened by disease and stagnated in a kind of limbo in which the future does not exist and the past is a vague remembrance with very banal contents. It is evident that we can discuss whether the author is really able to create the narrative environment and atmosphere intended, but without a doubt the whole effort is concentrated at the vertebral level—the bones, bodies, and spirits—of a reality in which human action tends to disappear, absorbed by the harshness of the landscape, in the fusion between the level of human beings and that of their world, which is already without a very recognizable form. It is not by chance that Leones's characters look for a book titled *Casa entre vertebras* (House among vertebrae), by a certain Wesley Peres, which somehow seems to have been prophetic of the disaster narrated in *Dentes negros*. Leones also tries to reinforce the expressivity of the theme with the use of photographs by Lívia Ramirez, black-and-white photographs of abandoned urban landscapes, free of any personal reminiscence. Nonetheless, the photos of emptied environments and anonymous spaces are unable to awaken the estrangement necessary to avoid their reduction to the referential. Thus, the writing also tries to absorb the materiality of the reality of things, tries to create a narrative space that is analogous to its own absence, as is said with respect to the apocalypse: "An event that exhausts all that which approaches it with the intention of translating it into images or words. An event directly proportional to its own absence. An event equal to its own absence" (Leones 2011, 55).[5] Nevertheless, from this perspective explained by the author, the novel still leaves much to be desired: the reference to the apocalypse is unable to alter the realist framework of reading, but rather only erases referential elements, distancing us a little from the trivial. But it does not exhaust anything: it does not even explore in depth this inverted path that is presented there, nor arrive at this desired point of exhaustion by giving reality and life to that which the words announce.

The Natural History of the Dictatorship[‡]

The growing authoritarianism accompanied by the escalation in violence calls for a reflection on the role of art and literature in the face of authoritarian memory, political violence and the continuous disrespect for human rights, which at the world level only appear to increase and worsen. Literature has always had an important role in bearing witness to these atrocities, which in a cold narrative of history are often reduced to the watered-down dimension of political events or commercially exploited in the media extrapolation of their more spectacular effects.

A current example of testimony in Brazilian fiction is the novel *K.*, by Bernardo Kucinski, which was originally published in 2011 and which gained broad international publicity. The novel contains a fictional account whose events occur in 1974, and it reconsiders the experience of the dictatorship from the perspective of a Jewish and Polish refugee who escaped Nazism and who experiences the disappearance of his daughter, a university student and militant of a leftist organization in Brazil. Kucinski, who is a retired University of São Paulo (USP) professor, a former advisor to President Lula, and a well-known political scientist, is inspired by the true story of the disappearance of his own sister, and he builds a historical relation that establishes a parallelism between German fascism and the repression of the Brazilian dictatorship, which sparked interest in the publication of the novel's German version during the Frankfurt Fair. Without entering a detailed discussion of this novel, let us

---

[‡] A previous version was published as "A história natural da ditadura" in *Lua Nova. Revista de Cultura e Política*, 96.

[5] The original version in Portuguese reads: "Um evento que esgota tudo aquilo que se aproxima dele no intuito de traduzi-lo em imagens ou palavras. Um evento diretamente proporcional a sua própria ausência. Um evento igual a sua própria ausência."

only observe that it is based on a simulated autobiographical documentary, supported by notes from a fragmentary diary about the disappearance of the narrator's daughter. Fictionally assuming the perspective of the father himself, Kucinski creates a complex and elliptical archival structure, framing his Kafkaesque plot around the fictional testimony of the pathetic efforts against the bureaucracy of power and in the face of that which remains unsayable and unexplained in textual evidence: the painfully predictable consummated facts of the daughter's kidnapping and assassination by agents of the dictatorship. It thus concerns a simulated testimony of well-known historical facts that gains its authenticity in the literary construction of the very constitutive flaw of subjective testimony, which is unable to expose its explicit content because of its submission to the traumatic structure, an impossible condition of experience in the face of historical reality. Ironically, in other contemporary examples, this same narrative figure clears a wide terrain for the fictional simulation of subjective trauma, not of its reality, but of its symptoms, which is easily associated with the ambitions of formal experimentation and commercial success. We do not question the historical importance of testimony as a heuristic figure in the appropriation of memories from political history, only the trivialization of its modus operandi, which causes literature to lose what it has gained after finding an authentic voice in declarations and accusations.

To open up another front of reading, we could begin with a reconsideration of the 2006 novel *História natural da ditadura* (A natural history of the dictatorship) by the São Paulo writer Teixeira Coelho, also a well-known USP professor and art critic. It concerns an essay-novel in five parts, or one volume containing five books, as the narrator himself says at the end of the novel. A vast autobiographical and memorialist material is explored by an analytical and essayistic discourse whose target is the political structure of the military dictatorship and the authoritarianism of the twentieth century in general. As in the previous example, there is a certain analogical construction among different repressive and rebellious moments, beginning with the emergence of German fascism, already addressed in the first book, titled *Portbou*, which discusses the death of Walter Benjamin in the city of the same name. Meanwhile, the Argentinian dictatorship is a theme of the second book, *Sur* (South), which talks about the author's friendship with the Argentinian artist León Ferrari and his denunciation of the crimes committed by the Argentinian military government. The third book, *30*, discusses the revolutionary and authoritarian violence in Italy during the 1970s at the hands of radical organizations such as Potere Operario, while in the fourth book, *Teoria da tristeza* (Theory of sadness), memories of the times in Paris under the impact of student movements are sown into a complex dialogue among these historical moments with references to works of Western art, from Tintoretti and Turner to Louis Malle and Visconti, and to concepts of political analysis, from Walter Benjamin to Giorgio Agamben.

It would be impossible for us to account for this myriad of threads woven by personal and subjective memory, whose anachronistic, discontinuous and decentered structure is one of the book's themes. Its own proliferating movement, in which the sentences always unfold from the middle, with the multiplication of subordinate clauses, decontrols and challenges the logical and rational sequence of the main sentences. In an erratic way, this movement of accelerated unfoldings delays the defined arguments in favor of suggestive and associative chains that allow for a mixing of memories and present thinking without closing the narrative and sequential structure. Thus, two clearly polarized levels are mixed: a personal and autobiographical memory that, like a long trip with many encounters, loves, experiences and passages, is mixed with lessons about philosophy, art history and political struggles, unleashing a theoretical discussion that in a certain way thematizes the conditions of possibility of its literary project. This other level is identified in the intertwining of political history and the different paths of biographical and autobiographical histories. The first-person narrator, often accompanied by his girlfriend, Ana M., is clearly an essayistic "I" undersigned by the author. The reality of the historical events is mixed with the fictional, or at least retold, stories.

But why do we consider it a book about the dictatorship? The author does not intend to be a protagonist in the struggle against the dictatorship; his testimony is rather from someone who has participated little or not at all in the political process, but who here tells the story of this periphery or line of flight of one who distances himself from the center of events. On the other hand, it is a story that continuously questions the logic of the dictatorship and of political revolutions, whether speaking of the 1930 revolution, Italian fascism or the Argentinian and Brazilian military dictatorships, by always trying to extract the structural figures of this constellation of power whose most remarkable nature apparently resides in its repetition throughout history. As a result of this analytical effort, the novel's narrative style, and the fluctuating themes addressed by someone who was not necessarily in a privileged position with respect to them, we wish to identify in this book an alternative to the testimonial account that has been protagonizing most literature about the military dictatorships in South America, and whose most recent representative is perhaps Bernardo Kucinski.

It is known that the "age of testimony"—in the words of Shoshana Felman and Dori Laub—begins, in a certain way, with the Eichmann trial in Jerusalem, in 1961, which allowed the declarations of eyewitness survivors who offered a much more emotional denunciation than at the Nuremburg trial, at the end of the 1940s, when only the objective presentation of documentary evidence was allowed. We have already commented on the characteristics of this new type of testimony and its relation to the exploration of trauma and to a culture of memory, and it is no exaggeration to highlight the importance and the impact of this figure that extrapolates legal and political limits and has left its clear mark on literature, cinema, and the whole entertainment industry. In addition to a scientific conclusion, the exposition of the facts was both technologically and rhetorically important. In this sense, during the Jerusalem trial the dimension of representation and the dimension of exposition merged: on the one hand, there was the representation of the bones in the legal forum (the term "forensic" has the same Latin root as forum); on the other, there were objects that "speak for themselves" in a language that science is able to make emerge as a kind of "language of things."

Weizman and Keenan accentuate this dimension of the paradigm, which explains the meaning of a forensic aesthetics precisely in the creation of a new regime of visibility that is asserted with a certain political force in the convincing of the public. It concerns a complex process that has technological aspects in its analysis of records, in addition to discursive and rhetorical aspects. The authors suggest that the process involves the rhetorical figure of prosopopeia, defined as speech in which the orator gives voice to inanimate objects (Keenan and Weizman 2012, 28). The French art historian Jean-Marie Mondzain[6] expands this analogy by discussing the double sense of the term "prosopopeia," which, according to her, means giving a face to the person and, at the same time, making what does not have a face or voice speak. This interweaving of word and image, of hearing and seeing, is in the Quintilian concept of "*evidentia in narratione*," that is, making visible and evident in narrating. In other words, it concerns a truth that is displayed and simultaneously asserted while spoken in a convincing way. It is this speech that inhabits the visible, that displaces the illusion of a presence, and converts it into an implicit message of the exposed that is immediately comprehended and understood by the interlocutor.

Returning to Teixeira Coelho's book, some of the structural and enunciative features that define its narrative may be characterized from the perspective of the rhetorical challenge posed by forensic aesthetics. Let us remember the singular structure of the novel, formed by five books, of which we have already mentioned four. The fifth has the same title as the novel, "História natural da ditadura" (A natural history of the dictatorship), which calls attention to its particular meaning. Reading this part quickly reveals that it is here that the structure is linked to the figure of the quincunx, five parts in which four form a

---

[6] See: Mondzain (2015).

square and the fifth is in the center, as in the five points of a die. This figure is classical and describes, among other things, a form of plantation, a gardening and irrigation technique, military formations, molecular structures, astrological figures and rhetorical forms. It is also a simple way to compose five parts, as occurs in the book, in which the central element in a certain way binds the other four. Teixeira Coelho's appropriation of the quincunx was inspired by the novel *The Rings of Saturn*, in which the author, the German Winfried Georg Sebald, adopts the figure of the writer and character Thomas Brown, who in the book *Garden of Cyrus*, from 1698, discusses the principle of the quincunx. The appropriation of this element from Sebald is not by chance, since the author's influence is present in many aspects of the novel, beginning with the title, which refers to the two books *After Nature* (2003) and *On the Natural History of Destruction* (2004), thereby reconsidering the Benjaminian idea of a natural history as an alternative to human history. Thus, as in Benjamin and Sebald, we encounter in the style of fictional essayism an effort to overcome subjective testimony in the analysis and interpretations of objective constellations. If the four points of the quincunx represent the four cardinal testimonial perspectives, the fifth demarcates a structure that is objective yet latent and invisible to the naked eye, which allows us to relate the singularities of the experiences narrated and the repetition of certain figurations apparently bound to tragic determinations: the enigmatic suicide, the guilty loss of the son or daughter and the temptation of power, among others.

The narrator does not let go of the subjective sensibility of observation and memory, but his writing is an exercise in objective interpretation, in which discourse is called to the real through inserted photos, facts and names, deictic indexes of a real that binds the narrative to a given time and space. Not by chance, a significant example is found in the Argentinian artist León Ferrari, a friend of the author who gives him a work as a present, actually a notebook with clippings collected during the harshest years of the dictatorship. Begun in 1976, the notebook was a collection of news reports in which assassinations and disappearances were made known indirectly, without politically motivated denunciation. When it was published, in exile, with only a few printed copies, the title was *Nosotros no sabíamos* (We did not know), which indicated a denunciation that in a certain way precipitates its content, as in a chemical process that leaves a hard coagulation obstructing the free circulation of words and signs. It is evidence whose strength is not to reveal something unknown, for we already know about what the book says, and therefore its attempt to include reality in the writing should not be confused with documentarism. It did not concern bringing reality to literature but intervening in the question by giving reality to these signs and committing literature to the challenge of absorbing and reworking the material traces of political crimes.

In addition to the aforementioned epistemological tension in contemporary culture between a testimonial perspective and a forensic perspective, between subjective empathy and the appreciation of a certain committed objectivism, there seems to be an analogous tension in a large part of literary and artistic production between an extreme in which a subjective voice faces violence, misery and injustice through the expressive appropriation of traumatic experience, and another extreme in which the remains, traces and objects gain voice and life implacably.

Chapter 2

REALISMS IN QUESTION

It is easy to see that the question of realism continues to be relevant in debates on contemporary Brazilian literature. In an article from the *Folha de São Paulo* newspaper on February 23, 2014, "Notícias da literatura brasileira do século XXI" (News about twenty-first-century Brazilian literature), a representative group of professors, researchers and literary critics face the question of the main tendency in contemporary literature with impressively different responses. The editor of *Ilustríssima*, Marco Rodrigo Almeida, proposes substituting Machado de Assis's idea of a "national instinct," which helped to characterize nineteenth-century Brazilian literature, with a "subjective instinct" as a magnifying glass of the main tendencies of the new century. Thus, the idea would be that, in contemporary literature, the national perspective as a fundamental question has been replaced not only by a subjective and autobiographical tendency, but also by a social realism with an autofictional approach in which a certain subjective perspective repositions the boundaries between the social and the individual, on the one hand, and between experience and referentiality, on the other.

It seems as though the argument raised by *Ilustríssima* in defending the importance of the term "autofiction" in current literary production, strongly questioned and refuted by most critics, ends up suggesting that the fictionalization of individual experience once again authorizes the literary treatment of historical experience in a manner supported by testimonial literature. If the testimonial initially defined a literature of the Holocaust, political repression and the periphery, today, its perspective is reproduced in a kind of subjective chronicle of everyday reality. We will not discuss, now, the problems with this shift nor assess the critical divide on this idea, but only observe that, at the same time that one insists on the relevance of autofictional writing, it seems that its intrinsic argument is based on the premise of a realism that, as a continuous backdrop, would offer legitimacy to the literary. To refer to realism implies the view that the justification for literature is found outside of it, if not in historical and social experience, then in the staging of individual and subjective experience.

It seems, therefore, that the question of realism—whether social, historical or individual—is directed toward a defense of the centrality of the literary experience for culture and for contemporary society. Additionally, it appears that realism, in its aesthetic commitment, represents a questioning of the role of literature today, and does not find its relevance in describing and characterizing a certain genre of literary fiction. Thus, it is coherent to understand the emergence of realism along with the concept of "the literary" at the heart of modernity in literature. This argument is found in Roland Barthes (1986) and in Jacques Rancière (2004), who both observed the coincidence between an autonomous writing without ontological or referential necessities and a transparent style without the support of a narrator's voice, as occurs in Flaubert's *Madame Bovary*. Realism in a certain way defines the "aesthetic regime" that according to Rancière characterizes modernity and is not in contradiction with the liberation of expressive signs, which indicated the emergence of modernism a few decades later. We will soon discuss the profound connection between realism and modernism, but first it is worth highlighting two other conceptions of realism that continue to have relevance for current debates.

The most well-known is the thesis by Auerbach (2003) in which realism can be identified since antiquity as the introduction of a colloquial and common reality—simple people and everyday subplots—in elevated genres, thus breaking with the poetic principles of Aristotle, who tied elevated and heroic contents to the genres of tragedy and epic, and human and colloquial contents to the inferior genres of comedy and satire. Auerbach observes the infraction of this poetic ethics in the Old Testament and in Homer's epic, and thus presents a definition of realism as a "modern" feature that spans more than two thousand years and persists until today in references to the common world, to recognizable reality, and even to that part of it which, being marginal and excluded, normally passes unnoticed. Of course, the novel in a certain way is the genre that historically will raise itself and establish itself on this material, as Ian Watt (1957) affirms by showing the consolidation of the nineteenth-century novel based on realism.

A third view can be found in Foucault (2002), in the privilege that he concedes to Gothic literature and to the writings of Marquis de Sade in the eighteenth century, for introducing an effect of fear and terror in literature and exposing a violence that had only been treated allegorically earlier. In discussing Sade's ideas on the novel, Foucault suggests that this Gothic capacity inaugurates the "modern" to the extent that it exposes the capacity of literature to interfere sensibly in the comprehension of reality. Such is the case, also, in contemporary fiction, in which the impact of the violence represented is an element often identified as realism.

There are thus at least three interpretations of the role and status of realism that continue to appear in the common sense of the concept today and offer a benchmark of definitions that, instead of having a fixed content, is inscribed in the boundaries between distinct and at times antinomic forces for understanding how realism functions. The first interpretation explains, for example, the Brazilian regionalist project of the 1930s novel, with clear realist inspirations in the social criticism that motivated it. Even so, regionalism was the bridge for the most successful development of modernist literature in Brazil, the works of João Guimarães Rosa and Graciliano Ramos. The second interpretation, whose main object is socially marginal realities lacking in political representation, attributes to realist literature a political role of denunciation and flagrant revelation. And finally the third interpretation, which has been identified as a transgressive reality of violence and barbarity, has come to characterize, in Brazilian literature, a new urban realism of the 1960s and 1970s, which made use of certain shock effects and of moral and expressive transgression. But in all of these three versions of realism that qualify specific moments in Brazilian literature, one recognizes an experimentation with form and literary expression that is akin to tendencies in modernism.

Fredric Jameson (2013) suggests in a recent study that realism cannot be understood except through the historical boundaries and limits that contrast it, on the one hand, with classical literature and, on the other, with modernism. Without specifically entering the historical discussion of realism, Jameson's approach does not abandon its temporal premise and thus does not let go of the historicism prevalent in literary historiography. It suggests a historical divide in European literature between the emergence of a specific narrative impulse linked to the representational ambition of realism and its dissolution in the prevalence of description in the late nineteenth-century novel, which leaves plot behind and clears the way for the affective dimension that characterizes modernist textual experimentation from the beginning of the twentieth century. It is from this temporal perspective that Jameson analyzes the "realist" genealogy, which is tied in a dialectical way between the power of narrative and the power of affect. Without making a radical distinction between these two facets, we can thus explain the antimony that defines realism as being between the transformative movement of the narrative impulse and the perpetual present of affect.

Jameson's argument is interesting for several reasons. In the first place, because it emphasizes the importance of affect studies for the understanding of realism; it shows the profound affinity between the realist project and its unfolding in modernism, such that it deconstructs the presumed antagonism between the two. Second, because it explains that the power of affect is directly linked with the "visual" and ekphrastic aspect of realist description, to the semantic load of a sensible dimension in the text that directly interacts with the bodily sensations deployed by the text. And finally, because it displaces the reading of realism from its historical affinity with a certain positivist epistemology and its representational presuppositions that for decades limited the comprehension of realism to an ideal of representation that was neutral and verisimilar.

With the insistence on the affective and therefore performative aspect of the text, we can without contradiction work on contemporary realist representations, abandoning any strictly mimetic requirements, and focus on their effects and affects from the perspective of a rhetorical force that not only convinces the reader, but boosts the veracity of the fictional account. In Jameson's analysis, this performativity is linked to the aporia between a merely chronological narrativity and what the theorist chooses to call *récit*, adopting the French term that denominates a narrativity with the weight of destiny or death. *Récit*, which means account, does not suspend the narrative sequentiality of historical or documentary fiction, but has more closed plots whose more circumscribed and determinant causality allows for an existential understanding of the actions and a stronger identification with the reader. In the same manner that one perceives here a temporal difference between two ways of narrating the story that will characterize the actual impulse of the realist narrative, Jameson distinguishes between a description subordinated to the temporality of the story, which only completes the setting with a semantic material that corroborates the overall meaning of the narrated, and another in which the described gains a discontinuous corporeal presence without necessarily referring to the plot supported by the narrative. Contrary to Lukács's disregard for description, in which he sees only a superfluous redundancy that threatens the didactic clarity of the narrative plot, Jameson understands the importance of affect in the corporeality of the text, something that can become evident with a force capable of interrupting the course of the story. The affective aspect is not subordinated to the meanings of the narrative, but is corporeally asserted in an interruption of the narrative that threatens the actual continuation of the story. This is why Jameson identifies the modernist text with this "perpetual" presence of affective description which, without a counterpoint in the narrative impulse, will deconstruct the realist project and lead literature down another path.

From Realism to Post-Realism*

When we speak of realism in relation to contemporary Brazilian literature, it is normally in tune with a continuation of the historical project of the nineteenth-century novel, and from the perspective of an incomplete

---

* A previous version was published in 2016b as "Do realismo ao pós-realismo."

representational project of the twentieth century, which still merits respect and attention due to the task of visualizing the marginalized, excluded and peripheral reality of Brazilian society, mainly in big cities. In both cases, one recognizes in Brazilian realism a representational project strongly motivated by political and ethical awareness, against the excluding injustices of an authoritarian society. In the 1950s and 1960s, when the narratives of neighboring Latin American countries were exploring the fantastic and magical realism, Brazilian literature was reformulating the commitment of the social realism of the 1930s novel in the urban prose of the 1960s. Meanwhile, in the 1980s, realism was always the main reference, despite a certain libertarian fervor of postmodern metadiscursive experimentalism.

Looking at contemporary production today, it is not difficult to identify examples of this continuity and revival in the reformulation of the historical novel in its different formats, such as in the proletarian novel *Inferno provisório* (Temporary hell), by Luiz Ruffato; in Paulo Scott's Bildungsroman novel *Nowhere People*; or in literature such as *City of God*, by Paulo Lins, and *Capão pecado* (Capão sin), by Ferréz, that dwells on the violence and social misery of big cities, whether in an ethnographic, documentary or testimonial manner. Within the context of this discussion, the concept of realism has expanded over the past few decades by more carefully considering the aesthetic dimension, that is, the effects and affects left by representation. Thus it has been possible to consider effects of realism that have accompanied literary and visual representation without necessarily contrasting them, and the concept of realism has begun to open itself up to the lived aspects of representation that are confused with real experience. Already in the 1960s and 1970s, the French critic and theorist Roland Barthes contributed with the seminal 1968 essay "The Reality Effect," and afterward with his interpretation of the insignificant detail in photography in light of the dichotomy between *studium* and *punctum*, in which *punctum* refers to the haptic and affective impact that destabilizes automatic and ideological interpretations of the communicated meaning.[1] In Barthes's reading, the influence of the essays by Jacques Lacan[2] on the "real" was very important, and the conception of an impossible lived experience at the limit of the "symbolic" has survived and been reformulated by the art historian Hal Foster (1994), in his book *The Return of the Real* as an aesthetic effect of trauma, a paradoxical traumatic realism that convincingly offered a theoretical framework of the shocks of the real in a postmodern media culture. For Foster, traumatic realism reconciles the two predominant

---

[1] See Barthes (1981).
[2] See Lacan (1998).

paradigms of the twentieth century: the *referential paradigm*, according to which the image refers to a reality outside of it; and the *simulacral paradigm*, in which an image refers only to another image. Based on the example of the *Death in America* series by Andy Warhol, Foster argues that the (impossible) representation of trauma created effects of a real that is strongly subversive to the symbolic stability of what is recognized as reality. From such a perspective, the image becomes an index or archive of this same impossibility and insinuates a higher referentiality accessible only in its remnants. Nonetheless, it has not only been through rupture and estrangement that the emotional and cognitive effects of representation have been considered. The affective dimension in the encounter between textual materiality and the body of the reader or viewer has been introduced as another field of exploration that, in a certain way, has evoked a modern metaphysical ontology that Rancière (2004b) called the "insensible sensation" (*la sensation insensible*), and that appears in a certain aesthetic atomism in the representational descriptions of the realist novel. Here is evidence, for Rancière, of the link between realism as a historical movement and the emergence of the "aesthetic regime," which for him offers a more adequate analysis of the phenomenon than the periodical-temporal concept of "modernity." It is by highlighting the impact of these sensible singularities on intersubjectivities that I suggest that there is, in effect, an affective realism in which the work gains reality by involving the subject sensibly in a dynamic unfolding of its actualization in the world.

It is worth observing here how the concept of realism contains, etymologically, a paradoxical ambiguity between philosophical realism, which before the Renaissance identified a universal reality behind the sensible appearances of phenomena, and realism in the history of art, which identifies the mimetic possibilities in the record of the resemblance created via representations. The same tension is at work today in the contemporary discussion of realism, not in the form of a Platonic universalism, except perhaps the case of Alain Badiou's *inaesthetics*,[3] but in the emergence of a metaphysics in which thought puts material stability to the test in a sort of material atomism that characterizes the aesthetic and in which the body of the subject is engaged by an indeterminate molecular vibration, an insensible sensation of this subjectless level of perception and affection that operates virtually in the work.

It is important to recognize the intimate relation, in the context of realism, between visual and textual representation, whose origin is found in the programmatic writings of Renaissance perspectivism, which were strongly influenced by classical rhetoric and later by the way that the actual concept

---

[3] See Badiou (2004).

of realism arises to characterize, in positive fashion, the painting of Gustave Courbet.[4] The visual metaphor is frequent in the programmatic writings of historical realism to idealize a certain linguistic transparency in realist description, which would be confused with automatism in its acceptance of the equivalence between spontaneous perception and visual description in realist settings. The relation between narrative and description has certainly been one of the crucial points in the debates about realism since the essay "Narrate or Describe?"[5] As previously mentioned, Fredric Jameson (2013) revived the dualism from 1936 between narrating and describing to make a distinction between the impulse to narrate, on the one hand, and affect, on the other, which he directly links to description. Realism would come to be understood based on this relation of antimony between the impulse to narrate and affect, which threatens the progress of the narrative due to the sensible and derivative absorption that accompanies it. In this dynamic contrast, Jameson manages to show the complicity between the realist project of the nineteenth-century novel and the modernist experimentalism that stems from the linguistic materiality of a descriptive autonomy which is already recorded in the works of Zola and Flaubert, and which makes way for the poetic experimentalism of the avant-garde.

For the time being, we will not delve into the continuity of historical realism, but rather first question another tendency in current Brazilian narratives, which seems to speak of a very concrete and recognizable reality of the everyday life of the Brazilian middle-class. In contemporary literature, a voice has appeared, often in the first person, which expresses itself in simple, everyday, colloquial language, distant from the experimentation with the expressive boundaries of language. It is a voice that expresses its own experience in a clear oral language, which easily arrives at the ears of the reader. At the same time, it can narrate a story whose development becomes fragmentary or elliptical, with absences and descriptive gaps. The direct simplicity of the testimony of its own condition is tested, therefore, by the complex narrative structure, which unbalances and intrigues comprehension. Oftentimes, direct speech is mediated by the manuscript, the letter or the diary, and in this way autoreferentiality, one of the most characteristic features of modern literature, is revived. By means of a writing that cites another writing, one reflected on the nature of the literary, in an unfolding movement in which process and experience became the center and object of writing. This metafictional writing highlighted its skeptical awareness with

---

[4] See Brooks (2005).
[5] See Lukács (1970).

respect to the possible illusions of objective referentiality, and the literary acquired autonomy through its distance from the communicative and representational functions of language.

Flávio Izhaki's novel *Tentativas de capturar o ar* (Attempts to capture the air, 2016) invites the reader to participate in a philological plot whose narrative is built upon a sort of police investigation of the genealogy of the novel itself. In other words, the manuscript and its story constitute the main theme and are confused with the novel written by Izhaki. The book opens with two prefaces that explain the detour from the initial project of biographical writing. Alexandre Pereira, the main author of the notes presented, has researched the life of a dead writer, Antônio Rascal, who stopped publishing after writing three novels that we are told were relevant to Brazilian literature. Pereira works on the biography of the enigmatic writer until he has a fatal car accident. The selected notes that he leaves behind are fragments of a search process which, edited and accompanied by prefaces and an afterword by another author, are confused with the book that we have in our hands. Thus emerges the story of an apocryphal manuscript that, rescued and presented in a fragmentary way, with a variety of styles and several authors, offers an elliptical and complex mosaic of the biographical story to be reconstructed. There is a blending of the story of Rascal's life and the relationship between the biographer and his own father, of biography and autobiography, prioritizing the account of the investigation, guided by the enigma of the writer's precocious silence and by the hypotheses about what would have motivated him to stop publishing. The inclusion of unpublished works by Rascal determines the direction of Pereira's research, for among them is a confession of a homicide committed by Antônio Rascal when he accidentally runs over a person and, instead of aiding the victim, he throws the body into a river. This revelation apparently intrigues the biographer, who thus finds a possible motive for the writer's silence. On the other hand, Pereira is unable to determine the truth of the incident and is not certain whether it concerns a confession or a fiction in the first person. For the widow and the editor, there is no doubt about the fictional character of Rascal's writings, but for the biographer they indicate a fact that could elucidate the life course of the biographee.

Among contemporary writers, Flávio Izhaki had already gained recognition in 2013 after the publication of his second novel, *Amanhã não tem ninguém* (Tomorrow there's nobody), which was considered one of the best of the year after it became a semifinalist for the 2014 Portugal Telecom Prize. The novel is about a petit-bourgeoisie Rio de Janeiro family of Jewish descent, and features a complex narrative structure with a great variety of points of view on the everyday events of characters from several generations. In *Tentativas de capturar o ar* is also highlighted the author's skill in constructing an elliptical and fragmented narrative, conducted in a direct and colloquial language in the first person, without hindrances to understanding or syntactical experiments proper to the linguistic work of modernist writing. We can thus observe how discursive legibility is reconciled with elliptic complexity and fragmentary incompleteness in the structure. It perhaps concerns the characteristic of a post-realist generation in which the demands of representational transparency and the modernist and postmodern skepticism in relation to the project of historical realism are reconciled. On the one hand, there is an oral discourse centered on the first person that expresses an everyday middle-class reality that is easily identifiable in its sociocultural characteristics. On the other, there is a discourse that is founded on a textualized world in which there are no longer referential illusions, and in which representation is always directed to other representations, creating a seductive game of resemblances and analogies. There is thus a realism that is not supported in descriptive representation and its fidelity in relation to the world, nor in the subversive project of the relation that characterized metafictional literature, in which denunciation pointed out the lack of ontological consistency in the world in detriment to the real force of fiction.

In post-realist literature, which in my view characterizes a significant portion of contemporary fiction, one observes a colloquial innocence of intimate enunciation, which in its narrative structure challenges the boundaries of the textual domain. In the case of Izhaki's novel, the indiscernibility between confession and fiction evokes the fatality of an event that escapes narration. The introduction of the autobiographical and of private memoirs, caused by the autofictional tendency in recent literature, is one of the devices of this particular realism, which only escapes textualism to the extent that it manages to make evident a life that is greater and different from the text. In Izhaki's previous novel, the underlying theme was weakness in the face of illness; in this one, it is the emergence of the reality of the crime and its confession that marks the boundaries of the fictional. It is the revelation of a reality outside of the textual domain that characterizes post-realist literature, a certain ethical resistance in the face of skeptical irony in relation to the representational constructivism of that which is considered real. Without demolishing the textual domain by way of rhetorical strategies, post-realism recognizes the need for certain pragmatic responses to the deconstructive games of interpretation. The devices are often found in personal memoirs, in autobiography and in a certain development of the main character's transformations. The recognition of rare details whose meaning can be narrativized but which interfere in the path of the subject is one of the features that characterize this search for patterns and resemblances that are stronger than discursive constructions. When the narrator or character acquires the ability to understand life's signs, which are different and stronger than the text, the structure of the coming-of-age novel is evoked, in the search for the capacity to make sense by writing the experience of these limits, highlighted by the traces of an objective force that intervenes in life.

Chapter 3

A PAPER WORLD—REFLECTIONS ON THE REALISM OF LUIZ RUFFATO*

> All of my books, in one way or another, deal with a single question: uprooting. This main theme is present in *There Were Many Horses*, is present in *De mim já nem se lembra* (They No Longer Remember Me) [...] and is present in the *Inferno provisório* (Temporary Hell) project. What happened was that in *Estive em Lisboa e lembrei de você* (I Was in Lisbon and Was Reminded of You), I expanded this perspective by accompanying the character, a Brazilian immigrant, abroad. Up until then, I had dedicated myself to understanding this process of uprooting inside Brazil. With *Estive em Lisboa e lembrei de você*, I began to take this new path, which in *Flores artificiais* (Artificial Flowers) I explore in depth.[1]
>
> Luiz Ruffato
> *O Estado de S. Paulo*, June 14, 2014

In the modern literary tradition, one of the significant features in the recognition of the new autonomy that characterized literature as distinct from the fine arts was metaliterature. The book appeared as an internal reference to the book, and fiction became the protagonist of fiction itself, in a recursion

---

* A previous version was published in 2016 as "Um Mundo de papel—reflexões sobre o Realismo de Luiz Ruffato."

[1] The original version in Portuguese reads: "Todos os meus livros, de uma forma ou de outra, tratam de uma única questão: o desenraizamento. Este tema principal está presente em *Eles eram muitos cavalos*, está presente no *De mim já nem se lembra* [...] e está presente no projeto Inferno provisório. O que houve é que em Estive em Lisboa e lembrei de você ampliei esse olhar acompanhando o personagem, um imigrante brasileiro, no exterior. Até então, havia me dedicado a entender este processo de desenraizamento dentro do Brasil. Com *Estive em Lisboa e lembrei de você*, comecei a perfazer esse novo caminho, que em *Flores artificiais* eu aprofundo."

that took literature as a theme for literature. This type of metafictionality has existed since Cervantes and Shakespeare and in countless examples from Luigi Pirandello to Jorge Luis Borges, at the height of literary modernism. The effect of metaliterariness, which was created when the book was represented inside the book itself, was interpreted as an unsettling interrogation of the boundaries between reality and fiction. It provoked an impression of a realized plot as a determining structure for the heroes in search of truth, and simultaneously fictionalized the contingent events of the real. One thus exalted the reality of poetry and narrative, whose strength could enchant the profane world, and at the same time, one casted doubt with respect to the conventional limits of fiction in the face of reality. In a way, it was this metaliterary effect that became synonymous with literariness, to the extent that it provoked an experience of autonomy that in modernity would identify its aesthetic reality.

In Luiz Ruffato's recent books, the author creates a peculiar metafictional game that seeks to take modernist logic in another direction, even though structurally, at first reading, it may be identified with it. In *De mim já nem se lembra*, from 2007, Ruffato supposedly rewrites the letters that his brother José Célio had written to their mother, Geni. In 2009, within the Amores Expressos (Love Express) editorial project, he published *Estive em Lisboa e lembrei de você*, a novel that is allegedly the transcription of a long interview, recorded in four sessions, with Sérgio de Souza Sampaio, a worker from the state of Minas Gerais who had migrated to Lisbon. More recently, in 2014, he published the novel *Flores artificiais*, which is presented as a transcription and partial edition of a long manuscript sent to the author by a Dório Finetto, who was also born in Minas Gerais and whose family apparently had ties to the Ruffatos, a relationship that would have motivated the engineer to send his writings to Luiz Ruffato in order for the latter to make use of "some themes." In the three examples mentioned, the author seems to let go of the "creator's" prerogative by alleging the existence of nonliterary documents that serve as a foundation.

The structure of *Flores artificiais* is very peculiar and caused a certain perplexity among critics when it was published. The preface explains the circumstances of the encounter between the two writers, the amateur Dório Finetto and the professional Luiz Ruffato, as a consequence of two previous experiences with recorded interviews and letters sent to the novelist, who on these occasions offered to rewrite, organize and edit the other's speech. There is then a reproduction of Finetto's letter, which had accompanied the manuscript and in which he recounts the depression he suffered for spending New Year's Eve at the turn of the century in his apartment in Rio de Janeiro after having lived more than twenty years abroad as a consultant for the World Bank. Part of the treatment recommended by his psychoanalyst had been to tell his own story by writing a set of short stories, all of them situated abroad and recounting encounters between Finetto and other characters in this part of the book, which is titled "Viagens à terra alheia" (Travels to a foreign land).[2] After eight stories, all of which were dedicated to Luiz Ruffato and the psychoanalyst Regina Gazzola, there is a "Memorial descritivo" (Descriptive memorial) of Dório Finetto's biography, written by Luiz Ruffato, who thus appears as the genuine author of this part, which was incidentally not approved by Finetto. It is not surprising, then, that such a complex construction has sparked readings that sought to show the metafictional game according to the modern standard of seeking the original manuscript, or else readings that saw the trick centered on the author's wish to disappear behind the appearance of the author-character Luiz Ruffato, who assumes the role of simple scrivener at the service of the true "authors," namely, the common people who live and experience the narratives that forge the raw material for the professional novelists.

Let us first discuss the fictional construction of the novel's references and then approach the singular inversion of the point of view, which introduces an insightful perspective of contemporary Brazil's inclusion in the globalization process. I will initially suggest that Ruffato applies the metafictional game in the opposite sense of the modernist experiment. Instead of highlighting the literary autonomy that characterizes modernity in general, he seeks another foundation for a contemporary realism that is no longer supported by descriptive verisimilitude but rather by the speech and writing of characters who are no longer represented literarily but appropriated and included in their own materiality, despite certain stylistic accommodations—"assunto demandando estilo" (a topic demanding a style; 10). As Finetto had requested, the writer "envernizou a trama" (varnished the plot) according to his "próprios predicados" (own predicates). It does not matter whether this game is real or fictional, whether the characters of these three books exist or not outside of the fiction, nor whether Ruffato himself, here, should be considered an author, an implicit author or a character, or all three things at the same time. For our argument, it is more interesting to question the shift that occurs within the metaliterary options offered by tradition to provoke an effect of realism as a result of the textual reference thus created. In other words, we can see in this experiment an effacement of the boundary between fiction and documentarism, which is understandable for a historical realism, even though the demand here is more radical because it suggests a writing committed to its object, in this case another discourse, with which it indicates a sort of essential and ontological bond, in a search for the truth.

---

[2] Perhaps inspired by *Viagens na terra alheia* (Travels to a foreign land), a book by Teixeira de Vasconcellos published in 1863.

In the novel *There Were Many Horses,* Ruffato creates an experimental style that mixes the deformation of expression with the mimetic verisimilitude of metropolitan reality, thus combining modernist freedom with realist constraint. The author includes textual fragments collected on the street from passersby, pieces of paper, titles of books on sale, statues of saints and other hard pieces of texts and words that appear as remnants of a reality that is not necessarily represented by the novelist, but rather included in its raw materiality in his text. I have previously characterized this technique as indexical realism,[3] which is certainly part of a contemporary tendency that operates within the impossibility of distinguishing clearly between reality and its images, representations and simulacra.

In the current version of the same appropriation of voices or textual fragments that belong to others, the inclusion of material and extralinguistic remnants no longer works. In this case, the possibility of realism exists as a result of a reference conceived as a kind of spontaneous, raw and vital language that palpitates behind its literary transcription. If historical realism was deeply connected to modern literature as an expression of a new aesthetic regime of art, as Jacques Rancière has shown,[4] Ruffato's project corroborates the contemporary tendency of reviving literary techniques that come from that which Rancière has called the regime of the image, to the extent that it seeks expressions that are ontologically determined by the solicited real. It concerns a realism preoccupied with the origin of the created image, its reference, and in this sense, it points out the question of truth, on the one hand, and that of its uses and effects, on the other. The insistence on the facticity of the narrated, the autobiographical references, the recurring documentary features, the thematization of the technique and of the process always subordinated to the content to be crystallized by the writer, all abandon the literary purpose, the literary as an aesthetic experience, in the name of a challenge and of a commitment to be kept.

The concept of a regime of art basically characterizes the relation between ways of thinking, of writing and the image and reality of a certain historical moment. It concerns a distribution of the sensible, Rancière says, that demarcates what becomes visible and sayable, but it is a concept always challenged by its own contradictions and by the tense relation that is established among the regimes. In Rancière's well-known analysis of modernity, a word that he avoids, he distinguishes between basically three regimes of art: an ethical regime, linked to an understanding of the image similar

---

[3] See Schøllhammer (2012).
[4] See Rancière (2009).

to Plato's understanding; a representational or poetic regime, based on the analysis developed by Aristotle of narrative poetics; and finally, an aesthetic regime, identified with the autonomy of the aesthetic, sensation and poetic effect in the art of high modernity, in the literature begun in a unique way with Mallarmé's poetry and Flaubert's narrative, superbly represented in the novel *Madame Bovary*, in which experimentalism and realism meet and are reconciled in exemplary fashion.

The three regimes should not be understood as an attempt at periodization: even though the aesthetic historically arises with more precise indications than the other two regimes in question, it concerns a metahistorical concept. If Rancière's approach is interpreted in dialogue with Erich Auerbach's analysis of realism in Western literature, one can recognize that, just as Auerbach detects indications of the nineteenth-century historical realism in the description of everyday life and of a common reality without nobility already in Homer and in the Old Testament, one can also recognize the descriptive details without narrative functionality that for Roland Barthes[5] were the indicators of a "reality effect," which characterizes the symbiotic relation between autonomy and realism in the aesthetic regime. Although Auerbach perceived a certain continuity for more than two millennia of the inclusion of common everyday details, Rancière interprets the same phenomenon in light of a process of democratization that, in breaking with the hierarchical principles of the classical genres, liberates aesthetic pleasure and broadens the scope of what could be seen and said in modern literature and could justify the centrality of the realist project. Rancière describes novelistic realism as

> first of all the reversal of the hierarchies of representation (the primacy of the narrative over the descriptive or the hierarchy of subject matter) and the adoption of a fragmented or proximate mode of focalization, which imposes raw presence to the detriment of the rational sequences of the story. (2011, 24)

One should understand the three regimes contemporaneously, existing with a certain simultaneity and being anachronistic to the extent that they make possible the coming and going of representational forms from different historical moments. In this sense, to speak of a revival of features of the ethical regime does not suggest a return to the classical forms of poetry, but rather the demand for another relation between literature and the world that extrapolates concepts of reality and truth in the slippery domain of contemporary literary

---

[5] See Barthes (1986, 141–48).

production. It is based on this perspective that what has been characterized as the "return of the real"[6] should be understood, not only as the appearance of works of art whose extreme expressions threatened to break with modern notions of representation, but as a broader media movement that mixes everything: reality shows and *cinema verité*, pseudodocumentarism and postautonomy, biographism, autofiction and self-help, traumatophilia, confessionalism and other random forms. Under the impact of this general tendency, the challenge for contemporary literature is more acute and the revival of the realist project becomes a minefield in which any well-intentioned movement can implode into sentimentalism and naïveté. To demand that words and stories be real and true is by no means a gratuitous gesture that requires much caution and that should be performed with the freshness of the unprecedented and the experimental.

The first approach to observe in Ruffato's writings, which has been present ever since his first short stories, in *Histórias de remorsos e rancores* (Stories of remorse and resentment, 1998) and *Os sobreviventes* (The survivors, 2000), is the appreciation of the colloquial and orality, which marks a certain regional speech richly supported by a far-from-casual semantics identified in historical, cultural, social and geographical features that are easily recognized. Here, Ruffato not only recuperates and values the realist and naturalist tradition of Brazilian literature, but also associates himself with the orality of the neorealism that characterizes, for example, the 1930s novel and the realism of the Northeast and of Rio Grande do Sul. It is important to observe, in this tradition, the shift in the realist ambition from the descriptionism of the outside world, which can be recognized through its effort to record reality objectively by employing scientific and quasi-scientific discourses for a literary representation that takes language itself as an object. It does not concern a description of the objects and actions of a world that the author observes, but rather a discovery of the language that already inhabits this world and that becomes the object of literary representation, a reference that offers the real possibility of imitation, since a word can faithfully imitate a word, even though this imitation or reproduction of the application of the word and of the unfolding of the sentence is now done in writing.

It is clear that this shift from the real reference to its linguistic expression is only one of the contradictions of historical realism and is part of the autonomy that characterizes the aesthetic regime. For Rancière, the liberation of literary expression from its determination by the rules of classical poetics, which define the ethical and representational regimes, is part of the political

---

[6] See Foster (1994).

democratization brought about by the revolutions of the nineteenth century. From the perspective of the ethical regime identified by Rancière in Book 10 of Plato's *Republic*, the word is, in its expressive materiality, ontologically subordinated to the idea in a state of thought and also to the sensible materiality of objects. In Aristotle's *Poetics*, one finds the basis of the representational or poetic regime in an elaborate hierarchical system of control that is masterfully expressed in the genres and their highly hierarchical contents. For characters and topics superior to those of the common people, the appropriate forms are tragedy and the epic; for the inferior or equal, comedy and satire serve. The novel arises precisely at the same time as the emerging prevalence of these human and ordinary contents of the realist everyday life, which for Erich Auerbach[7] already constitute the germinal *mimesis* of modernity. The aesthetic regime was a result of the liberation of the contents of the hierarchical system envisaged by the representational system; any content could gain nobility of form, which used to be restricted to a select few. Thus, the formal liberation of literary expressions was accompanied by a democratization of the contents, which linked the political to the aesthetic in an intrinsic way as a new visibility for what was recognized as real.

When Ruffato and some of his contemporaries revive the precepts of historical realism, they rekindle the contradictions of the modern regime, such as its tensions with ethical and representational elements, which were never totally abandoned. In modern literature, a representational foundation in the organization of narratives has always been maintained, even when free of plots and despite the expressive possibilities in the materiality of language. Likewise, the belief in a Platonic ideality of the principles that guide the logical rationality of actions also accompanies modern and contemporary literature and art as an insistence on something more true and real behind that which semiotically seems to be mere convention. In the representational regime, the most important principle is the fictional and narrative structure; language and poeticity occupy the main position, and with them, the predominance of the text over the image is consolidated. In the aesthetic regime, the image is asserted over the text, and description over narrativity. Even though the literary or poetic would define literature as different from the other arts, it finds its strength in the expressiveness of words and no longer in its structuration as narrative plot. In the aesthetic regime, words are no longer solely instruments to give voice to a previous truth; they encounter truth in their own expressivity, and not only in the elaboration of a story. The argument here is that precisely this point is

---

[7] See Auerbach (2003, 547).

the unresolved contradiction between the representational and the aesthetic, between the prevalence of the plot and the autonomy of poetic expressivity, which already in the beginning of the twentieth century motivates a turn in historical realism by giving emphasis to the reference of oral language. There arises the writing of a realism that can now let go of seeking the right balance between narrative and description, a difficulty discussed by Lukács, to point out the expressiveness of the oral as a creativity that upgraded the conventional figurativeness of the lexicon and sensibly dynamized the story in its molecular structure.

The strategy of appropriating the oral is easy to recognize in the neorealisms of the twentieth century. In Brazil the prime example is the orality of Guimarães Rosa's writing, which illustrates another aspect of this device, namely, the abundant application of common and proper nouns, elements of language that draw linguistic convention to the indexes of beings and concrete things, which appear as a kind of deictic reference of discourse in the same way that a dialectal sign can mark a nonarbitrary relation to the user of conventional language. One perceives that underlying this merely representational strategy underlies an insistence on the possibly "real" links between the word and the thing, between language and the world, as if it were somehow possible in literature to review the initial act of Adamic naming and, in a performative way, qualify what is specific to this reality, safeguarding the trademarks that identify and designate it, on the one hand, and fictionally and aesthetically recreating its virtual process, its becoming and its potency, on the other. For Ruffato, an author given to the construction of large narratives, such as the five-volume proletarian novel *Inferno provisório*, regional orality carries with it a certain cultural and social identity that is expressed in the syntactic dynamics and in the unfolding of the colloquial reasoning, reconstructed in writing, that has always been a feature of his singular regionalism. The option, in his most recent books, for an apparent strategy of direct appropriation of the text or discourse of the other should be taken as a deepening of this contradiction in contemporary realism.

If the "reality effect," for Roland Barthes, was a consequence of the insignificant and apparently superfluous detail, Ruffato seeks a reality index in the relation constructed between the figure of the author and his relation to the text. The appearance of the author as a character is, in this case, more than an autobiographical feature or a symptom of autofiction, following the contemporary Brazilian style. It rather seems to be part of a series of details that tend to suspend the fictional pact and create a continuum between documentary trademarks and fictional devices, an indistinguishable zone between literary creation and its circumstantial references. If the author thus introduces his place in fiction as that of an operator of the reality indicated, it is worth questioning, upon second reading, the physiognomy of the reality in question. One should recall that the main character is the narrator, Dório Finetto, supposedly the author of the initial manuscript, which is presented by means of eight accounts that all together is called "Viagens na terra alheia" (Travels in a foreign land). Finetto speaks in his own name and says little about himself, and the accounts are ruled by encounters with other characters with whom he meets in his travels around the world and whose stories he is interested in telling.

In the first short story, "Uma história inverossímil" (An unlikely story), we are introduced to Bobby, or Robert William Clarke, in a narrative that even includes descriptions of Finetto's childhood and youth. Bobby was born in Southampton, but he spent his childhood in Brazil and, after a life marked by his participation in the English colonial wars in Africa, ends up in Juiz de Fora as an expert in rat poison, looking in vain for the woman he loves. In the short story "O presente absoluto" (The absolute present), the narrator meets a French woman in Buenos Aires—a married woman, mother of two children and a retired teacher—in search of the sensuality of tango. And in the "El Gordo" (The fat man) account, the encounter is with a Uruguayan who bears a heavy secret about the fact of being abandoned by his father, who escapes to Brazil under the pretext of escaping the dictatorship, but is actually chasing after another woman. In "Comer sushi em Beirute" (Eating sushi in Beirut), the theme is also the dictatorship, this time in Argentina, and the story is told by the political scientist Marcelo, who escapes from his fatherland in the first days after the coup and never returns. Most characters are foreigners who, like him, tell Finetto about their experiences away from home. In the chapter "Susana," Alexandre tells the story of the beautiful Portuguese woman Susana Souza, who seems to flee from her own beauty and, after a traumatic experience as a volunteer in Africa, ends up disappearing in Timor, probably committing suicide. Others, such as the woman from Havana or the hotel owner from Hamburg, are people he meets in travel encounters that catalyze the narrator's reflections and mirror, each in its own way, questions tied to exile.

Thus a double perspectivism is constructed in which the dialogical relation between the narrator, Finetto, and his encounters reflects the global experience from the point of view of one who is neither at the center of the hegemonic view of Western culture nor at its Brazilian periphery, where the narrator loses his identity after two decades of working abroad. A fictional image of reality is thereby created that is not the external view of one who describes Brazil from the outside, seeking its exotic distinctions, nor a reflection of the perspective of the Brazilian traveler who compares what he or she experiences abroad with that which he or she normally undergoes because of some desire for inclusion or for an "attraction of the world," as the writer Joaquim Nabuco formulated. Here, Finetto's encounters are mostly with people who live through exile at the periphery of the periphery. Since the accounts are centered on travel encounters, fiction becomes a way to think of the world, to imagine and project the globalized world and abandon the particular contentions of a realism bound to the local or national experience.

In this sense, one is faced with a particular case of what has been defined as a "novelization of the global,"[8] a counterpart of the globalization of the novel, which is characterized by the production of images of a globalized world. Instead of producing or reproducing the universal discourses of adventure based on a perspective of a world to be conquered, *Flores artificiais* reflects a totally shattered, fragmentary and dysphoric global perspective of characters in deep despair and in search of some affirmation in a life in which neither nationality nor cosmopolitanism offer plausible identities. In a situation in which a large part of Brazilian literature exhibits its resourcefulness in the globalized world with a high frequency of travel stories, of adventures and conquests in foreign countries now within reach of a competent and well-off traveler, the stories narrated by Ruffato capture the side of solitude and uprooting in travel encounters. Already in the novel *Estive em Lisboa e lembrei de você*, the story focused on the disappointment of the main character's great expectations in the face of the naïve expectations of a worker from the Minas Gerais countryside. Even so, the fictional account of the narrator's experience created the image of a Portugal with an unrecognizable geography and a somewhat predictable idea, within the Brazilian popular imagination, of the characteristics of this country that is so close to the history of Brazil. In *Flores artificiais*, the recognizable literary geography disappears, and the encounter with others takes place in a spatial topography and an uncertain geography whose descriptive characteristics become phantasmagorical, sustained only by random traces of the plotted dialogues and by a very discrete narrative of the actions of characters who nonetheless reflect reasons and affects that are convincing and moving.

Everyday Life[†]

The innermost recesses of private life have gained an extensive dimension in the contemporary as a result of social networks and the massive presence of

---

[†] A previous version was published as "Inventário do real" in Ángela Maria Dias; Sterfania Chiarelli Atores em Cena.

[8] See Siskind (2014).

electronic media in the mediation of everyday life, such that it profoundly alters the boundaries between the private and the public. This section will tackle some of the consequences of this transformation and discuss its reflections in literary and artistic representation in Brazil. The main hypothesis is that the new media affect the actual concept of subjective experience and create a third dimension between the private and the public, a dimension of cybernetic privacy in TV, blogs, the Internet, tweets, messages and so on, which is neither private nor public in the traditional sense. In this third dimension, intimacy appears in the construction of a subjective avatar made for selective exposure in the digital forum of a network of contacts among friends or followers, in which everything can really become public, that is, accessible to the anonymous general public. It is in the construction of this cybernetic privacy that a certain "autopoiesis of the self" is created, which grants a new legitimacy in the revelation of the intimate dramas that traditionally were only revealed in a confessional way in diaries and memoirs. Thus, a new sphere of the immediate is produced that is characterized by the penetration of representations, fictions, images and other material from a public imagination that makes present a historically different raw material for a subjective experience of the contemporary.

The Argentinian critic Josefina Ludmer (2007) supports her diagnosis of the postautonomous state of contemporary literature on this transformation of the private sphere in the face of the privileged space of modern literature:

> The post-autonomous literatures of the present would escape "literature," would cross the boundary, and would enter a real-virtual medium (in matter) without outsides, the public imagination: in all that is produced and circulates and penetrates us and is social and private and public and "real."[9]

It concerns a new experience of everyday reality that, according to Ludmer, absorbs all past realisms and effaces the boundary between the subjective and the historical as well as between fiction and reality. Ludmer coins as already mentioned the word "realityfiction" to describe this effacement of the autonomous and delimited spheres, of the economic, the political, and the cultural, for in forgetting the literary, everything is reduced to raw material for the

---

[9] The original version in Spanish reads: "Las literaturas postautónomas del presente saldrían de 'la literatura,' atravesarían la frontera, y entrarían en un medio [en una materia] real-virtual, sin afueras, la imaginación pública: en todo lo que se produce y circula y nos penetra y es social y privado y público y 'real'."

public imagination. Gone are the specificities of the literary, its identitarian attributes, its value and its critical and liberating force that depended on its autonomy. Ludmer's perspective is very skeptical and identifies tendencies in contemporary writing both within what is still symbolically characterized as "literature" and in a writing that has no intention of being literary but simply appears in and out of the available formats and media. One can argue whether Ludmer is right to eliminate the question of literary value, but the issue here concerns describing the change in status of its everyday material. For Ludmer, the private is no longer distinguished from the public imagination, the factory of the present, in which the difference between reality and fiction is not pertinent. Before pursuing this argument, it is interesting to recall the way that the everyday enters literary theory and mainly how it identifies a traditional sense of realism in literature and art.

At the end of his classic book on Western realism,[10] Auerbach identifies his critical operation of describing realism in its varied formats with a shift in the confidence that he perceives in the modernist works of James Joyce and Virginia Woolf, in which "the great exterior turning points and blows of fate are granted less importance" than the common reality of common characters and not so extraordinary situations (Auerbach 2003). Thus, the raw material is the human in its most immediate and ordinary sense, which in Aristotle's poetics could only appear in inferior genres such as comedy and satire. Contrary to this ethical hierarchy that determined a certain form and a specific genre for a content identified with the everyday, without any pedagogical value and without any ideality, Auerbach performs his reading against the grain of a traditional understanding of modernity and its close relation to the literary realism of the eighteenth and nineteenth centuries. Auerbach shows that the poetic and artistic recognition of the human everyday already appears within the Western cultural cycle at its origins in Homer's epic and in the Old Testament, which suggests a representational subversion of the ethical hierarchy of classical poetry that already prefigures its historical realization with the representational autonomy of modernity. Auerbach disconnects the understanding of realism identified with a language of representational transparency and ties its definition to the importance of the everyday, in which one assumes a density of the real that can absorb on a level of day-to-day life, in the stuff of routine, in the immediacy of historical experience.

> In any random fragment plucked from the course of life at any time the totality of its fate is contained and can be portrayed. There is greater

---

[10] See Auerbach (2003, 547).

confidence in syntheses gained through full exploitation of an everyday occurrence than in a chronologically well-ordered total treatment which accompanies the subject from beginning to end, attempts not to omit anything externally important, and emphasizes the great turning points of destiny. (Auerbach 2003, 547–48)

Here we touch upon the possibility of understanding the everyday as a texture of day-to-day reality that resists representation and that, for Auerbach, is somehow understood in an essential way not as an ideality but rather as a materiality of life, an object for what in German is called *Alltagsgeschichte*, a story of everyday life. The sociological analysis of modernity exalts the conversion of life into routine as a result of massive serial production and its bureaucratic organization, and the followers of Max Weber and Marx tend to identify the everyday with alienation.

The theoretical discussion on the everyday has become more profound since Henry Lefebvre's *Everyday Life in the Modern World* (1968), Agnes Heller's *Everyday Life* (1970) and Michel de Certeau's *The Practice of Everyday Life* (1980), in which day-to-day life is analyzed not only in the dimension of the alienated routines of the everyday but also as a resistance against the system's control from above and also against the conformity from below. For Certeau, for example, the everyday constitutes a "network of antidiscipline" that resists the microphysical devices of power described by Foucault, for instance, in the body regime and the dominant ideology, and is expressed in the creativity of groups and individuals who are against hegemonic control. Thus, according to Certeau, the everyday cannot be confused with a depoliticized conformity but rather must be recognized by its material and affective potential. Either way, whether interpreting common life as resistant matter or as dense conformity, one perceives a division that originates in the distinction formulated by Wilhelm Dilthey and later by Walter Benjamin between *Erlebnis* and *Erfahrung*, which reflects two distinct ways of understanding the process.

The term *Erlebnis* is translated as lived experience and expresses the prereflective stimuli of the outside and the inside, such that it is associated with the notion of *Lebensphilosophie*, or philosophy of life, which exalts immediate lived experience in detriment to the rational access of experience, which means the historical and cultural integration of these impressions within meaningful schemes. Lived experience describes the pragmatic responses to the shocks of external and internal stimuli, while experience in general denominates an integration of the sensory stimuli into a narrative network of meanings. In Benjamin's interpretation, modern life favored the increase of sensory stimuli in lived experiences and impeded their integration into historically significant experiences. In other readings, such as, for example, those of Roland Barthes, it becomes clear that the appreciation of this everyday content may vary. In the seminal article "The Reality Effect," Barthes alleges that the description of superfluous, useless and functionless details within fictional and narrative constructions somehow makes present the very fabric of the real. This reality is self-sufficient and does not need a function because it becomes an index of "having-been-there," a material reminiscence that in the book *Camera Lucida* appears to be interpreted in its affective dimension as a "touch" of the image, which here is called *punctum* and possesses the power to distort the interpretive process of decodification through *studium*.

Jacques Rancière has critically discussed this parallel in Barthes, mainly challenging the Barthesian postulate of *punctum* as an immediate and sensible affect that simply testifies to the reality of the real. From the libertarian perspective of encountering in the idle excesses of description a path toward an alternative world, Rancière for his part highlights an opening up to another life through the intimate relation to the everyday in the same short story Barthes discusses: "A Simple Heart," by Flaubert.

> The barometer is not here to attest that the real is the real. The question is not about the real, it is about life, about the moment when "bare life"—life normally devoted to look, day after day, whether the weather will be fine or bad—takes on the temporality of a chain of sensuous events that are worth writing. The idle barometer expresses a still unheard-of poetics of life, evincing the capacity of anybody, for instance Flaubert's old servant, to turn the routine of the everyday into the depth of passion, whether it is for a lover, a master, a kid or a parrot. (Rancière 2009)

Directly inspired by Auerbach, Rancière analyzes the appearance of the everyday in realist description as the potential for idleness, the right not to do anything, an equality of the sensible that should not be identified with bourgeois abundance unless it is intimately tied to the autonomy of literature and thus to the possible democratization that it has caused. It is somehow in this dimension, in the autonomy of the sensible and the affective, that modernism revives what in modern realism appeared in excessive description and its "reality effect."

In his aforementioned book on realism, Frederic Jameson (2013, 35) emphasizes the same relation between the autonomy of description in realism, which is always in an antinomical tension with the narrative impulse, and the expressivity of affect in modernism, which in a certain way suspends this tension in favor of the representation and setting of a realism of affect. For Jameson, the modernist text is already virtually present in realist description and explores its visual and performative potential, its affective dimension, which is capable of suspending the impulse to narrate and bringing the experience of the story to the objectivity of the textual object. Description somehow seeks not only to give an image and a form to the phenomenon, but also to efface the difference between the thing, its object and its textual expression. This hallucinatory mechanism formed a part of the aesthetic understanding of avant-garde movements, for example, in André Breton's idea of a real that gives access to the imaginary, a surreal object that in a way pointed to a fascinating ambiguity in the everyday, its ambivalent familiarity and sinister strangeness. Hal Foster (1995, 7) shows how this indistinction between the real and the imaginary is related to Freud's theory of *Das Unheimliche*,[11] which is elaborated in the essay of the same name. One should recall that Freud's concept is the combination of the "familiar," *Heimlich*, and its negation, *Un*, translated as the uncanny, and involves the return of the familiar—an object, an image, an event—which has become strange due to a repressive process. The consequences of this return are, for Freud, the indistinction between the real and the imaginary, the confusion between the animate and the inanimate and the submission of physical reality to psychic reality or of the referent to the sign. In Freud's theory, this ambiguity creates anxiety in the face of repetition. This is how Breton imagines the "marvelous" in the two Surrealist manifestos as a path to freedom by means of art, and it shows very well the importance that the everyday object gains in surrealism as a lever for a dialectical experience in which reality is denaturalized and potentially loses its alienated enchantment. The same idea appears in the 1960s in the situationist concept of *derive*, in which a small shift in urban routines, executed, for example, by the *flâneur* drifter, can destructure the micropower of urbanism.

In the contemporary, the everyday no longer presents the dynamics of this ambiguity, for through virtual reality an indistinction is produced between referent and image that may be illustrated by a quote from the novel *O paraíso é bem bacana* (Paradise is really cool), by André Sant'Anna:

> Mané didn't even know that in the Caribbean Sea there is a group of islands that is called Caribbean. But, even so, Mané was walking on a beach in the Caribbean. Mané was holding hands with Pamela, who was wearing a skimpy neon-green bikini, and with Jasmine (Page 32 from the imported *Playboy* magazine), who was wearing a skimpy bikini, which imitated the skin of a hot-pink Bunny, with a glued hot-pink pompon.
>
> There were many coconut trees on that Caribbean island.

---

[11] See Freud, "The Uncanny." Available at: https://web.mit.edu/allanmc/www/freud1.pdf. Accessed July 5, 2019.

The sea was very blue and clear on that Caribbean island.

Pamela stops and looks into Mané's eyes, Jasmine embraces Mané from behind and grabs his, Mané's, cock.

Mané rubs his hand on Pamela's pussy, over the bikini. Jasmine takes his cock, which is big, black, hard and full of veins, and pulls it out of his shorts. (2006, 88)[12]

Sant'Anna consciously and radically explores the effacement between representation and reality. With him are balanced the two great paradigms of the twentieth century, as Hal Foster (1994) would say: the referential and the simulacral. In the former, the image points to a reality outside itself, and in the latter, the image is itself a reality. If this relation corresponded to the confrontation between social realism and the Pop movement, Foster introduces, in the example of Andy Warhol, an artist who is at the same time referential and simulacral. That is what happens in Sant'Anna's writing: representation is suspended by the devices of repetition. The sign does not represent its referent but turns it into a symptom of the impossibility of this relation, this "failed" encounter with the referent, which makes it automatically repeat the failure. From Foster's perspective, a traumatic realism is defined here in the synthesis of the two paradigms, whose most notable effect is the conversion of the public sphere into a pathological sphere in which private fantasies are confused with public reality. The exposure of these fantasies in Mané's everyday life is one of the narrative threads of the novel, another being the delirium of the football player who is hospitalized and seriously wounded after exploding in a failed attempt to become a suicide bomber and martyr during a game of his club team, Hertha-Berlin. With his body torn apart, wounded and ripped open, the

---

[12] The original version in Portuguese reads: "Mané nem sabia que no mar do Caribe existia um grupo de ilhas que se chama Caribe. Mas, mesmo assim, Mané caminhava numa praia do Caribe. Mané estava de mãos dadas com Pamela, que usava um biquíni reduzido verde fosforescente, e com Jasmine (Página 32 da Playboy importada), que usava um biquíni reduzido, que imitava a pele de um coelho cor-de-rosa fosforescente, com um pompom cor-de-rosa fosforescente colado.

Havia muitos coqueiros naquela ilha de Caribe.

O mar era muito azul e transparente naquela ilha do Caribe.

Pamela pára e olha nos olhos de Mané, Jasmine abraça Mané por trás e pega no pau dele, Mané.

Mané passa a mão sobre a boceta de Pamela, sobre o biquíni. Jasmine tira o pau negro, grande, duro e cheio de veias para fora da Bermuda."

character becomes a metaphor for the contemporary public sphere, or as Mark Seltzer defines it: "The spectacular public representation of violated bodies has come to function as a way of imagining and situating, albeit in violently pathologized form, the very idea of 'the public' and, more exactly, the relations of bodies and persons to public spaces" (1998, 35). Wound culture, Seltzer says, is a traumatic culture in which the main symptom is the effacement of the distinction between the private and the public, between inside and outside and between the individual and the collective. Thus arises a strange collective subjectivity, a mass psychology that can explain the strategic importance of violence and suffering in contemporary media, for trauma has become a psychosocial valve of negotiation between the psychic and the physical, between the imaginary and the real, between representation and perception and between the private and public orders of things. Perhaps that is why there exists a generic bond between a literature dedicated to the testimony of violence, pain and zones of human suffering and misery in society, on the one hand, and on the other, that which has gained a new confidence in the expository exploration of the private sphere of an everyday that is more than ordinary and common.

An example of a narrative situated in the sphere of personal issues ruled by actions with immediate intersubjective reach is the novel *Toda Terça* (Every Thursday), by Carola Saavedra (2007), in which the character Laura explains to the psychoanalyst Otávio:

> My week had been just like all my others, at least in the past few years. I had slept until late, woken up in a bad mood, taken a bath, drunk a cup of coffee, and played with my cat. Depending on how I felt, I cleaned the house a little or went to the gym. I almost always turned on the TV, sometimes just to hear the indistinct sound of the TV. Other times I sat there on the couch flipping through the channels. Most of the shows were for housewives and students who don't have anything else to do. I rarely went to the university. The truth is, besides visiting Otávio every Thursday, most of the time I didn't do anything. (13)[13]

---

[13] The original version in Portuguese reads: "A minha semana tinha sido como eram todas as minhas semanas, ao menos nos últimos três anos, dormira até tarde, acordara de mau humor, tomara banho, bebera uma xícara de café, brincara com o gato. Dependendo do ânimo, arrumava um pouco a casa ou ia à academia, quase sempre ligava a televisão, às vezes só para ouvir o barulho indistinto da televisão, outras vezes eu ficava ali, sentada no sofá, mudando de canal de dois em dois minutos, a maioria dos programas eram para donas-de-casa e estudantes que não têm mais o que fazer. Raramente ia à faculdade. A verdade é que, além da visita que fazia a Otávio toda terça-feira, na maior parte das vezes não fazia nada."

The whole plot develops indirectly between the two main characters, Laura and Javier, and is based on imperceptible changes in their day-to-day practices, which are always attracted by small erotic intensities which imperceptibly shift that which seems to be most solid in a world organized around the private sphere and its possible intersubjective contacts. The plot, which intertwines several stories and characters in a complex way, unfolds almost exclusively in the private sphere, relating everyday happenings in an apparently stable reality supported not only by their routines, but also by the described inventory of events and by the perspective that every character projects on their options and on the connections that determine their individuality. On the other hand, a new possibility arises in microscopic shifts in the actions and behavior involving this everyday, which unfolds and shakes the stability of reality by pointing toward a vast array of possible futures and possible worlds as a result of apparently meaningless differences. For example, the character Javier, who lives in Frankfurt, begins a relationship with the German woman Ulrike motivated by his attraction to the similar name Ulrica from a short story, which he is coincidentally reading at the time, about the encounter between the Norwegian Ulrica and the Colombian Javier. The insightful reader knows that it concerns the "Ulrica" short story by Jorge Luis Borges, in which two characters meet by chance in an English hostel and experience an erotic moment under the spell of the place and of a sound coming from the forest that is interpreted as a wolf's howl. There are no more wolves in England, Javier observes, but at that exact moment, the incident makes evident an infinity of parallel worlds that are similar or different only due to tiny shifts, an idea that Borges cultivated from the philosophers Blanqui and Democritus. At every moment, in every act, the world can unfold in a parallel world in which, yes, there are wolves despite everything else remaining the same. For Javier, there also arises the awareness that there is a freedom that consists of doing something different than what he normally does, such as, for example, while sitting on a park bench in Frankfurt and watching a group of Japanese tourists, his realizing that he can also buy a plane ticket and wake up the next day in another country and in another world.

> So easy to leave. And it was the first time that this thought, always present, always around, took shape in all those years. And then, also for the first time, the suspicion, that, maybe, the most important thing was still to come, that the most important thing was still on the other side, always about to happen. (Saavedra 2007, 126)

In the book *Malaise dans l'esthétique*, Jacques Rancière (2004a) proposes that there are two main tendencies in contemporary aesthetics. One gives continuity to the romantic aesthetics of the sublime and identifies the radicalness of art and literature with the singular power of presence, appearance and inscription that extracts common experience from its banality. It is possible to understand the collapse or traumatic inversion of the public and private spheres as an expression of this view of a radical experience of the sensible. The second tendency described by Rancière is close to relational art, and the argument here is that, in a certain intimist literature also, the strategy is the rearrangement of the objects and images that form the world in common with the already given reality. By producing small shifts, situations are created that modify our view of and relation to the collective. Based on the private sphere, new realities are suggested with almost imperceptible subtlety, or as a latency of something that eventually may come to happen or exist. In the novel by Carola Saavedra, this latency is the narrative razor's edge on which the characters, without heroicism or dramaticity, are balanced, and the minute descriptions create situations, at times hilarious and at times pathetic, of the everyday that are capable of modifying the characters' attitudes with respect to the common world and thereby their actions and destinies.

Notes on Postautonomy

The contemporary in Brazilian literature resists strict conceptualization. Continuity and renovation seem to be notions that do not clarify what defines and happens in current fiction. Realist tendencies are mixed with modernist experimentation without offering a framework that is justified in light of the diversity of production today. How to differentiate contemporary from modern literature? And what really characterizes the contemporary in literature? From a certain perspective, and speaking of fiction written in Brazil in the past decade, this discussion has been centered on the representative role of literature, something that is not surprising since the national literatures of modernity arose within a program of national cultural identity formation. Without a doubt, this mission is still significant for the Brazilian national narrative, and every effort is valid to stimulate the emerging creative expression on the part of the population that is at the margin of the canonical circles of production and consumption of literature and art. The literature produced in the country is evidently not representative either as the spokesperson of the population or as a portrait of the reality that it offers to its captive audience. Written mostly by middle-class male authors who are white and college educated, according to research by Regina Delcastagnè,[14] its representativeness is the same or

---

[14] See: Dalcastagnè (2013).

worse than the political representativeness of the elected congressmen. From the point of view of representativeness, there is a repressed demand for voices, statements and accounts from the population in its real condition of diversity, and it is not strange that the literary market has shown itself to be receptive to this demand. Perhaps the survival of the passion for the real in Brazilian fiction at the beginning of the century is explained in light of this question. The preference for urban underworld themes, a certain literary documentarism and variations on the historical novel or (auto)biography are only a few of its preferred formats.

There is, however, another approach to the current situation of the realist genre and the evolution of its forms based on two examples from very different novice writers. Both combine the revival of formats that represent a certain realism with a referential construction that may be defined as ethical by the way in which it extrapolates the aesthetic autonomy that is characteristic of modern literature. The first example is the autobiographical novel *A Número Um* (The number one, 2015), by Raquel de Oliveira, and the second is the book of short stories *O Sol na Cabeça* (The sun overhead, 2018), by Giovani Martins (2018). Both cases concern novice writers revealed in literary workshops and events outside of the commercial book circuit that appeals to talents in favelas and peripheries of the city of Rio de Janeiro. Both are also the result of the FLUPP Literary Festival project,[15] which since 2012 has been bringing a new visibility to the emerging literary production in the peripheries of Rio de Janeiro. In this sense, both fit within so-called marginal or peripheral literature, even though they are very different and particular. Praised by figures such as João Moreira Salles and Chico Buarque de Holanda, the book by Giovani Martins was published by the Companhia das Letras publishing house, and the rights were sold to eight countries. The most powerful editorial machine in Brazil launched this new "phenomenon" with the same marketing savvy that earlier made the novel *City of God* a success in the Brazilian literature of the 1990s, which opened the doors to new voices testifying to the shadowy side of Brazilian reality: exclusion, marginality, crime and violence.

For the French philosopher Jacques Rancière, modernity in literature is part of the emergence of the aesthetic regime in art and occurs as a result of a rupture with representational poetics, which had been consolidated since antiquity in the principles defined by Aristotle's poetics. Rancière's surprising argument is to propose that the literary realism of the nineteenth-century novel, with the privileged example of *Madame Bovary*, by Flaubert, provides a

---

[15] Translator's note: FLUPP is the acronym for the Festa Literária das Periferias (Literary Festival of the Urban Periphery).

sample of representativeness supported by the autonomy that will characterize what, instead of the "modern" label, he prefers to call an aesthetic regime. The autonomy of the aesthetic, according to Rancière, makes the representativeness of realism distinct in relation to the representational regime defined by Aristotelian "mimesis." Realism introduces a rupture with the hierarchical principles that intrinsically determine the relations between content and form. Thus, autonomy in its modern version breaks with an ethical basis of values that marginalized the human, the everyday and the common experience in genres such as comedy and satire. It is based on this reading that Rancière consolidates the association and the fundamental relation between historical realism and experimental modernism, both expressions of the freedom that accompanies the literary with aesthetic autonomy. Every reality here gains its legitimacy, every emotion has its own dignity and can be represented without necessarily being accompanied by moral judgments, and all print literature can circulate and be read by anyone.

Our interrogation after this brief summary aims to understand the representational and aesthetic consequences for literary writing in the contemporary condition, which is characterized by the postautonomy that accompanies the critique of aesthetic value. If one of the features of the contemporary is the suspension of aesthetic autonomy, here are three interpretations of the consequences of such a transformation, which are not necessarily separated antagonistically but which emphasize distinct features of their consequences. The first reference that is asserted in this reflection is the diagnosis of the contemporary proposed by Josefina Ludmer, who as of 2007 began to publish manifestos of postautonomous literature on websites whose very existence was an important basis for understanding a new regime of production and visibility in this postautonomous writing. The object of Ludmer's analysis was primarily Argentinian authors at the beginning of the twenty-first century, but it was easy to see that her aim was to understand the contemporary condition in general. Her central argument is that there has been a collapse of modernity's constitutive separation between public and private space, in part a consequence of media proliferation and its superimposition on reality, which created a sort of eclipse between reality and fiction, between public and private and between media dream and individual imagination. Ludmer thus gave continuity to the more skeptical post-structuralist tradition, such as, for example, the works of Jean Baudrillard on "third-order simulacra," which evoked the abolition of the difference between representation and reality and a true decline of the real. If one suspends the symbolic relation to death in modernity, Baudrillard emphasized, death appears anywhere; and if one suspends the recognition of reference, everything can become a reference and reappear anywhere as a symptom of its disappearance.

For Ludmer, the critical instrument proposed was *speculation*, an affirmative activity shared by writers and critics committed to challenging and further effacing the difference between the abstract and the concrete, between the public and the private.[16] Ludmer's postcritical strategy was "to speculate," that is, to affirmatively "mirror" or fable a territory of literary and artistic production imbedded in what she calls public imagination. Thus, in a sort of fictional approach, she offers a critical position for a production of presence within the condition that she considers the "factory of the present." If everything is representation, then representation suddenly becomes concrete and material; if we eliminate critical distance, then reflection loses its dialectics and may become positively part of the production of reality. The privilege of authorship is lost with individuality, and everything passes through the intimate and private as through a public sounding board in which nothing is personal and nothing is foreign. *Meaning* is confused with affect and *experience* is absorbed in the intensity of living in the present. This dimension of immediate *presence* has played a decisive role in Ludmer's argument. The anachronistic allowed for the dissolution of historicity in the immediacy of lived experience, and its presence marked a large part of its contemporary expression, with a frequency anchored in the biographical and autobiographical subjectivity that allowed for the present reliving of any historical fact in memory, and offered this same experience in reading and critical commentary.

With this diagnosis of postautonomy, the analysis of literary production is no longer interested in the quality of the singular work except as a symptom of a condition of presence in the "realityfiction" that oscillates freely between the historical and the melodramatic, between the collective and the individual, between the media and contemporary literature and art. In this demolition of the modern hierarchy of "high and low," of "good and bad taste," of "writing well" and "writing badly," the criteria of the quality of the work and its aura

---

[16] Ludmer revises this diagnosis in 2010, in "Notas para Literaturas Posautónomas III" (Notes on postautonomous literatures III): "In the case of reality and fiction (a previously bipolar opposition), one could imagine the fusion as follows: one pole eats the other, fiction eats reality. In fact, fiction changes status because it encompasses reality until becoming confused with it. It is possible that the development of technologies of the image and media has liberated a form of the imaginary in which fiction is confused with reality (which Beatriz Jaguaribe develops in her book on the 'shock' of the real, *O choque do Real: estética, mídia e cultura*. Rio de Janeiro: Rocco, 2007, p. 119). The result is realityfiction, which is not made of the two, it is not a mixture, a *mestizaje*, a hybrid, or a combination, but a fusion in which each term is immediately the other: reality is fiction, and fiction is reality" (https://josefinaludmer.wordpress.com/?s=notas&submit=Buscar).

or authenticity disappears. Ludmer militantly asserts the necessary disappearance of aesthetic value, but does not come to recognize the return of the oppressed in another value with ontological resonance. From the perspective of Jacques Rancière, however, contemporary literature is still in the aesthetic regime and criticism should insist on exploring the potential of the autonomous. In dialogue with Rancière, and as the second position to mark the postautonomous, one may nonetheless consider the rupture of the autonomous in the contemporary in the form of a reintroduction of the ethical hierarchies that determined the premodern regimes. It is true that one should not confuse the three sensible regimes of the author with a historiographic periodization of literature. The regimes are simultaneous, not successive, and it is possible to reinterpret what the contemporary means in literature and art as a certain return of the hierarchical relation between content and form that characterized the ethical regime. In clear opposition to Josefina Ludmer, one perceives the emergence of a truth value, a certain ontology connected to the value of lived experience and to collective or personal identity.

The best example is the recent appreciation of testimony in literature, of the content authorized by the "locus of enunciation" (*lugar de fala*), whose reflection is asserted in the contemporary, not only in the case of subaltern voices but also in every form of identitarian discourse. In the discussion on the testimonial literature of the 1980s and 1990s, from Spivak to Agamben, a certain post-structural solipsism threatened the critical value of testimony, since it was understood as inaccessible due to a discursive blockage in the case of subalterns and to the repressive mechanism of trauma in the case of statements from Holocaust survivors. The symptoms of this impossibility were detectable in the gaps, the alliterations, the discursive failures and the silence that were all exalted as evidence of testimony. Thus, some contemporary writers sought veracity through a combination of stylistic experimentation and a discursive evocation of individual trauma. Nonetheless, Djamila Ribeiro[17] finds the necessity of understanding the "locus of enunciation" to be pertinent, but not as a personal right, since this term in Ribeiro's understanding expresses the need to enlarge a place for the collective and not for individual experience. The way that this collectivity is narrated is one of the great questions that is recognizable in the writing of authors such as Carolina Maria de Jesus and Paulo Lins. In the former, it is expressed in the anonymous weight of extreme poverty and hunger that guide her diary, and in the latter as a fictional project ethically inspired by collective history and a testimony elaborated through a conscious political conversion of his ethnographic research.

---

[17] See Ribeiro (2017).

The book by Raquel de Oliveira is a fascinating autobiographical statement by a woman whose biography is confused with the marginal history of the Rocinha favela in Rio de Janeiro and the development of organized crime in the 1980s. The girlfriend of Naldo (Ednaldo de Souza), or Pará, Raquel recounts her private and passionate relationship with the drug dealer who introduced heavy weaponry in the community and began another stage in organized crime. Naldo was illiterate and gained power after the death of Bolado, who was accidentally struck by machine gun fire. He assumed leadership of the drug trade with the blessing of Denir Leandro da Silva, or Denis, who, after being arrested in 1987, continued to be the crime boss in Rocinha. It was Denis who became famous in Rio de Janeiro for publically supporting his parallel power by giving spectacular interviews in the media. Naldo ended up attracted by the seductive celebrity status that finally caused his extermination during a confrontation in the Grotão favela, in 1988, as part of the so-called Operation Mosaic II. All of this can be read in Raquel's story, an autobiographical account that is woven as an allegory of the history of the community, the city and the country. This collective quality of her testimony is evident in unique moments of her novel, such as when she tells how she was forced into adoption by her grandmother, who delivered her to the local *bicheiro*,[18] and raised as a prostitute in one of Rocinha's whorehouses. Raquel escapes this destiny, but offers an original statement by a woman raised in poverty and trained in contravention. In the novel, she tells how, after Operation Mosaic II, for a time she inherited the command of Naldo's gang, surviving the life of crime and drug dependency, and after treatment began to write in order to deal with the burden of this memory. Is it true? Fiction? It is not possible to draw a clear dividing line, since Raquel writes with ease in an intense melodramatic vocabulary of love, sex and friendship, not always in this order but always related to the crazy life, drugs and death, separated by the romantic evocation of bravery and comradery. Nevertheless, none of this removes from the narrative the veracity of the character's difficult experience, which is here fictionally reinvented, or the importance of her remarkable statement.

In the book by Geovani Martins, there is a very different example in the stories written with skillful language and scathing sentences inspired by a certain canon of Brazilian urban fiction from the 1970s. The combination of a young 26-year-old author's perspective with preferably first-person characters, who bring to the narratives the experiences of thousands of black and poor youth who grew up in the favelas and peripheries of the big city, represents a

---

[18] Translator's note: A *bicheiro* is a head of a gambling ring.

great achievement for Brazilian fiction. We hear the raw voices of this youth, whose orality permeates the language of an author stylistically trained in her readings of literary tradition, and who thus renews the traditional representational role of literature. But that is not all. In the narrative, Martins creates a space of risky topology that is marked and territorialized, as if in a minefield, by boundaries, impediments and contentions. A narrative time of flight and a journey is asserted here that, as Miguel Conde would say,[19] creates its own rhythm as it reflects the lightness and also the detachment that characterize a generation which is without a defined place or a guaranteed direction and is uncertain of an effective social inclusion. A space-time is asserted in the style of short sentences and a syntactic skill that evokes Nigel Thrift's tentative definition of the concept of *nonrepresentational*: "a geography of what happens."[20] For Thrift, it concerns a certain theoretical style of *speculative realism* that descriptively recreates the material, corporal and affective making of its object with components that are not exclusive to the theoretical effort but rather belong to the performative dimension of the nonrepresentational, of fiction and critical reflection simultaneously, which should be highlighted here as the third feature of the contemporary. The nonrepresentational aspect is expressed in the flow and affluence of the everyday, Thrift says. It is a descriptive construction of the experience underway and is thus deeply connected to affective corporal and precognitive dynamics. In addition, it is of a pre-individual nature and encompasses modes of perception that are not supported in the subject, but that reflect practices of subjectivation in the body and its interaction with the materiality of the world.

In conclusion, the three characteristics of the contemporary here described evoke values of authenticity, veracity and experience, of a notion of reality present in literary writing, which suspend not only representational realism but also the autonomy of the aesthetic driven by the urgency to intervene, by the feature of the collectivity that is superimposed on life stories and asserted through its performance in an affective presence of spaces and times of realities at the limits of the representable.

---

[19] "Na travessia, ele inventou o próprio ritmo" (On the journey, he invented his own rhythm). http://www.suplementopernambuco.com.br/edições-anteriores/72-resenha/2071-na-travessia,-ele-inventou-o-próprio-ritmo.html.

[20] See Thrift (2007).

Chapter 4

BRAZILIAN LITERATURE AND THE MARKET

In 2002, the Chilean writer Roberto Bolaño published in the *Las Últimas Notícias* (Breaking News) newspaper a short story titled "Sobre la literatura, el Premio Nacional de Literatura y otros consuelos del oficio" (On literature, the national literature award, and other tricks of the trade), on the occasion of the granting of this award to the writer Volodio Teitelboim. With his usual irony, Bolaño, who certainly does not hold much respect for his colleague Teitelboim, author of a biography on Pablo Neruda, suggests that a national award would soon be given to Isabel Allende, the post-boom best-seller writer par excellence, before they give her the Nobel Prize. Bolaño's argument is irresistible:

> Made to choose between the frying pan and the fire, I choose Isabel Allende. Her South American glamor in California, her imitations of Garcia Márquez, her unquestionable courage, her writing that goes from the kitsch to the pathetic and that somehow resembles, in a Creole and politically correct version, that of the author of *The Valley of the Dolls*, a result which though seemingly difficult, is far superior to the literature of born public servants such as Skármeta and Teitelboim.[1]

If authors earlier faced the schizophrenia of opting between critical recognition and market sales, Bolaño's satire is directed at the fact of encountering, in the beginning of the twenty-first century, a new agreement between

---

[1] The original version in Spanish reads: "Puesto a escoger entre la sartén y el fuego, escojo a Isabel Allende. Su glamour de sudamericana en Califórnia, sus imitaciones de Garcia Márquez, su indudable valentia, su ejercicio que va de lo kitsch a lo patético y que de alguna manera la asemeja, en versión criolla y politicamente correcta, a la autora de El valle de las muñecas, resulta aunque parezca difícil, muy superior a la literatura de funcionários natos de Skármeta y Teitelboim."

literary awards and honors, on the one hand, and the public's preferences, on the other. In the 1980s, this dilemma was still discussed in Brazil as a conflict between the market and the critical recognition of a generation that arose in the previous two decades. For the first time, the market thus seemed to promise growth indexes that were enough to make it possible for the fiction writer to professionalize, and in the 1984 essay titled "Prosa literária atual no Brasil" (Current literary prose in Brazil), Silviano Santiago advises that "the Brazilian novelist today needs to professionalize before becoming a professional of letters" ([1984] 1989, 29),[2] that is, the writer needs to be prepared to face the dangers of a new commercial relation to the trade so as not to succumb to the temptation of assuming the digestible formats of market taste and abandoning the literary project and the quality standards of coherence and experimentation inherited from modernism. Six years later, in 1990, Santiago comments on the Law of Markets, warning that the writer comes to

> produce a text of good quality, but that is unable to escape redundancies (excesses) and predictable elements (clichés) [...] He sought to forge an original albeit precarious path, for he had to pass through the field of enemies to have them as allies [...] Another thing is certain: in the 1980s there was a gradual abandonment of the great political event as a backdrop for poems and novels (Santiago 1990, 74–75).[3]

In today's light, it is curious to note that several of the authors who emerged at that moment, the truly anonymous members of the canon at the time, quickly overcame this dilemma and assumed the leadership of the national market in terms of the possible and modest measures of sales in its category (Adult Literature) and of the critical reception of fictional prose. In some cases, they forged the formal molds for a new generation of successful writers that became consolidated at the end of the 1980s and beginning of the 1990s, such as, for example, João Ubaldo Ribeiro, Antônio Torres, Ana Miranda, Patrícia Melo, João Gilberto Noll and Bernardo Carvalho. It would nonetheless be unfair to accuse this generation of succumbing to the temptation of the best

---

[2] The original version in Portuguese reads: "O romancista brasileiro de hoje precisa profissionalizar-se antes de se tornar um profissional das letras."

[3] The original version in Portuguese reads: "a produzir um texto de boa qualidade, mas que não consegue escapar às redundâncias (excessos) e aos elementos previsíveis (clichês) [...] Procurou forjar um caminho original, ainda que precária, pois tinha de passar para o campo dos inimigos para tê-los como aliados [...] Outra coisa é certa: na década de 1980 houve um abandono gradativo do grande acontecimento político como pano de fundo para poemas e romances."

seller; among novelists, at least, even those who tried did not manage to obtain a significant response from readers. It is true that some authors managed professional independence, but most still could not let go of other jobs, and the expansion of the market was never realized in accordance with the optimism at the beginning of the economic recovery envisioned by the Plano Real (Real Plan). Whoever accompanies best-seller lists of literary fiction knows that the appearance of Brazilian novelists is rare, for they are normally dominated by translations of big international names such as, for example, Dan Brown, who during the past has been able to clog this list with up to four titles simultaneously.

The first observation, then, is that even the writers who proposed commercial goals were unable to encounter a format capable of competing with the globalized sales market. Not even authors such as Patrícia Melo, whose initial success with *The Killer* placed her on *Time Magazine*'s list of Latin American personalities of the twenty-first century, could do so. Her solid sales are explained by the consolidation of the formula already approved by her master Rubem Fonseca, a formula that has become the canon of suburban literature with themes of suspense and crime. The initial success of the first historical novel by Ana Miranda, *Boca do Inferno* (Mouth of hell), also arose from the same apprenticeship, combined with the talented marketing by Companhia das Letras, the leaders of an ever more competitive publishing market. It is true that some writers tried new market sales recipes, which include commissioned books that are popularly themed such as *Plenos Pecados* (Sheer sins) and *Literatura ou Morte* (Literature or death), or prereleases of chapters in booklets, as in the case of the novel *Inferno*, or on the Internet, as in the case of *Casa dos Budas Ditosos* (House of the fortunate Buddhas), by João Ubaldo Ribeiro. It is also clear that writers appeared with a purely commercial vocation and achieved a certain success within traditionally popular genres, such as the detective novels by Luiz Alfredo Garcia-Roza, the conspiracy fictions by Ivan Santana or the historical satires by Jô Soares, whose "unauthorized" autobiography—*O Livro de Jô* (The book of Jô)—is the most recent and successful attempt to reach the best-seller lists.

But these are not the writers who characterize the market. If we speak of the actual book market, schoolbooks predominate with almost half of sales (47.5 percent in 2019),[4] followed by religious books with one-fifth of the pie (18.8 percent in 2019), and finally the adult literature (5.7 percent), youth literature (3.2 percent) and children's literature (9.2 percent) segment, within which we find that all narrative and fictional writing occupies a modest 18.1 percent.

---

[4] https://snel.org.br/wp/wp-content/uploads/2020/06/Produção_e_Vendas_2019_imprensa_.pdf.

And within this segment, of greater interest for literary criticism, we should recognize that nobody has managed to encounter wide public acceptance on the scale previously managed by Jorge Amado, except for, obviously, Paulo Coelho, whose case deserves a separate evaluation. The great national best sellers are writers such as Augusto Cury and Padre Marcelo Rossi, whose books range from self-help to existential religious meditations and encounter a very wide acceptance among readers.

For novelists and prose writers in general, we observe only that the commercial threat against the freedom of form was never realized. Instead, the Brazilian literature market has been transfigured during the past 20 years as it has sought to expand its sales base in large bookstores, in cheap collections of classic books and through a proliferation of fairs and literary events as well as through a greater integration in the mass media, such as on television shows, as a result of the greater dialogue with the expansion of the cinematic sector. The 1970s generation has earned its place in the canon, at times in the rows of the "immortals" of the Brazilian Academy of Letters, and has become established with awards and inclusion in the required readings of public schools, the great market sales lever. In Brazil, there is no Isabel Allende, no Laura Ezquivel, not even an Osvaldo Soriano, and much less a Roberto Bolaño, writers who in the Latin American context cleared the way among best sellers after acclaimed masters such as Gabriel Garcia Márquez and Vargas Llosa. No one has arisen in the place of Jorge Amado, who from this perspective is missed, for no one offers a literature that aims to introduce a global view, not even idealized or folkloric, of Brazilian reality.

Despite the modernization of the publishing market, its economic reality is critical today. The growth of the book market only accompanied the general economic growth of the country until 2005, and as of that year the book market stagnated until 2009, while growth was disappointing. Between 2009 and 2014, the decline of the share of book sales was a reality in the years of Dilma's government, when growth in gross domestic product showed clear signs of exhaustion.[5] From 2014, the retraction of the book market has accumulated a drop of more than 20 percent in 2015–16 while government purchases presented an increase of 13.8 percent, which balanced the general market drop with a reality of slight growth in nominal revenue (0.73 percent) in 2017. In the year of 2018,[6] the drop in sales were 10.1 percent and

---

[5] Source: *Produção e vendas do setor editorial brasileiro*. Câmera Brasileira do Livro.

[6] Produção e vendas do setor editorial. Ano base 2018. Camera Brasileira do Livro. https://snel.org.br/wp/wp-content/uploads/2019/04/Apresentacao_pesquisa_ano_base_2018_imprensa.pdf.

considering sales to the market only religious books had a small growth of 1.1 percent. From this economic perspective, it is good to remember that the fiction and poetry segment as a whole is less than a fourth of total sales. With the surprising exceptions of novels such as *My German Brother* (2014), by Chico Buarque, which had market success in 2014, and of reeditions of old and new classics such as *At Your Feet*, by Ana Cristina Cesar, *Claro Enigma* (Clear enigma), by Carlos Drummond de Andrade, or *Toda Poesia* (All poetry), by Paulo Leminski, which suddenly and unexpectedly earned significant sales, the Brazilian sales champions are found in the documentary or semi-fictional genres, such as in biographies, historical reports and chronicles by writers such as Ruy Castro, Fernando Moraes, Caco Barcellos and Arnaldo Jabor.

The success of Paulo Coelho, obviously, is an exceptional situation to be considered from this perspective. First of all, since the beginning of his literary success, after the publication of *The Diary of a Magus* (1987), he has foregone local or national references, which were so important for Jorge Amado, and also shied away from an experimental or even conscientious handling of his mother tongue, inasmuch as he writes in a neutralized and translatable Portuguese that has found a public interest in a kind of New Age cosmopolitanism, with its recipe of combining smooth and agile narratives, a global imaginary that mixes religious and mythological references and anecdotes without much historical commitment and self-help existential philosophy. Although Coelho was an active member of a very outspoken hippie movement in 1970s Brazil as a songwriter for Raul Seixas, his first fictional steps were taken during the 1980s at a moment when the ties between national literature and an identitarian project of national culture suffered a rupture imposed by the ironic distance typical of postmodern deconstructions of the romantic and even the modern or progressive roots of the national cultural project. Coelho was not part of this critical discussion, and instead placed his fiction in another sphere with no national or culturally specific markers and with no real demands for, or challenges to, the expressivity of the Portuguese language.

The commercial success of Paulo Coelho's books arises in this vacuum, and his writing becomes an example of a Portuguese language that does not take responsibility for contemporary reality in the broadest sense, since his stories are often placed in whatever geographical context is required. This political and cultural indefinition is not only caused by a global redefinition in which the traditional question of commitment to national identity no longer points to an adequate response, but is also a conscious choice for a thematic and linguistic translatability that appeals to an easy identification worldwide. A frequent comment about Coelho is that his Portuguese often sounds like a simplified translation from some foreign language, and often that his works in translation are better than the originals. This strange loss of linguistic identity is apparently a consequence of a fictional universe in which imagination does not depend on the exploration of the boundaries of one's own language and in which language is never the place where this reality is explored. On the other hand, this observation does not explain Coelho's massive sales but only the fact that he is never taken as an example of a truly Brazilian literature.

The Spy, by Paulo Coelho

Ever since the novel *The Alchemist*, published in 1988, the commercial success of Paulo Coelho has been unquestionable. His books, 34 in all, have been translated into 80 languages, and the sales are astronomical, totaling today more than 210 million copies in 170 countries. No Portuguese-language author, not even Jorge Amado or José Saramago, surpasses these numbers. Today, any release by Paulo Coelho counts on a marketing machine that guarantees the propagation of simultaneous editions in several languages, and the author maintains the regular rhythm of one published book every two years. Paulo Coelho has received international awards, such as the Crystal Award, and since 2002, he has been a member of the Brazilian Academy of Letters.

In his recent novel, *The Spy* (2016), the plot is constructed around the figure of Mata Hari, the Dutch dancer executed by French troops in 1917, at the end of the First World War, under the accusation of being a spy. Born in 1876, Margaretha Gertruida Zelle became Mata Hari after a failed marriage to Rudolf John MacLeod, with whom she had two children and who took her to Indonesia. It was during the years spent on the island of Java that she was inspired to create the figure of Mata Hari. When she returned to Europe, she moved to Paris, where she was successful in bohemian circles due to her seductive dancing and exotic costumes. Legend has it that the dancer was the lover of several personalities at the time, including some soldiers and politicians of different nationalities. That was how she ended up becoming involved in an international intrigue of espionage and counter-espionage, which Paulo Coelho fictionalizes in the first person—in the voice of the protagonist—based on legal documents, news reports and now accessible letters. The author informs us right at the beginning of the book that it is "based on real events," and his approach is identified with "literature-truth," a popular and very current mixture of documentarism and fiction whose ambition is to place literature at the service of truth by the empathetic power that would reveal to the reader the subjective intimacy behind the historical facts. It is not the first time Coelho employs this artifice. In the novel *Eleven Minutes*, he alleges that he initially departed from a manuscript of memoirs belonging to the Brazilian prostitute whose story he tells.

The author certainly has some skill for the commercial project that he proposes to undertake, but the result is not convincing, and the novel at no time places its own premises to the test. It becomes clear from the start that Coelho interprets his heroine through clichés, trying to take advantage of the contemporary feminist moment. He presents the main character as an independent and free woman, innocent of the accusations that led her to death by firing squad, only trying to survive in a man's world in which the most efficient weapons were her body, her seductive intelligence and her capacity to listen to her many lovers. "Her only crime was to be an independent woman," the author asserts, in big letters, on the back cover, winking in an evidently opportunist way to the contemporary female reader that he hopes to seduce.

Without a doubt, Paulo Coelho identifies with the character, and the use of the first person during the main part of the novel emphasizes this yearning for understanding. Unfortunately for the reader, the result lacks psychological depth, just as the description of the historical context of the First World War does not present the complexity that one would expect from a historical novel. The first-person narration is a dangerous instrument, and the "autofictional" feminine testimony does not overcome the exteriority of the author's masculine perspective. The innumerous catch phrases about herself eliminate the interest that the plot in itself would offer. Instead of a complex and fascinating woman who interacted with important artists and politicians of her time, there is a narrator whose voice is flat and buried by self-help proverbs. This becomes explicit in the encounter with Picasso and Modigliani, in which the latter gratuitously offers Mata Hari the following pearl of wisdom: "Know what you want and try to go beyond your own expectations" (Coelho 2016, 71). Thus, the exchanges of instruction manual wisdom empty the novel, which also not so incidentally bears the weight of many biblical quotes and mythological references, not to mention the street smarts, which have come to be the author's trademark.

The project of creating a literary defense for Mata Hari could be interesting, but, despite the similarities between her story and the Dreyfus case, Coelho is no Zola, and the question is not really whether she was guilty or innocent. It is difficult to identify the key to success of Paulo Coelho's literary formula; he is not a creator of suspense plots in the manner of a Stephen King or Dan Brown, nor does he have the creative freedom of J. K. Rowling or Gabriel García Marquez. What he offers is a sports coach's philosophy of life, which does not challenge literary skill or stretch the boundaries of language beyond the commonplace.

Blood-Drenched Beard, by Daniel Galera

It is well-known that the writer Daniel Galera (b. 1979) is one of the great young hopes in contemporary Brazilian literature. His novels and short stories were all promising in the complete sense of the word, competent examples of a developing narrative and seeds of an embryonic fictional capacity whose maturity was still difficult to see. In a way, Galera was a victim of his own talent, for he writes so well that what in other writers would be a satisfactory result in his case appeared beneath his real promise. He was part of a group of writers from Porto Alegre that arose on the Internet in small virtual publications. He participated in the *Livros do Mal* (Books of Evil) publishing project, in collaboration with Daniel Pellizzari and Guilherme Pilla, in which he published his first two books, *Dentes Guardados* (Stored teeth, 2001) and *Até o Dia em que o Cão Morreu* (Until the day the dog died, 2003). He debuted with Companhia das Letras, in 2006, with *The Shape of Bones*, which received critical acclaim, and he participated in the Amores Expressos (Love Express) project with the award-winning novel *Cordilheira* (Mountain range, 2008), which was situated in Buenos Aires. Ever since his first works, it was perceived that Galera was endowed with a craftsman's capacity in fiction, with good plots and a fluent style, despite being closed in an overly juvenile universe and in a pop culture treated without much distance. For all these reasons, the recently published novel *Blood-Drenched Beard* promised to be a qualitative leap in Galera's career, perhaps his first great novel, and at least, judging by its 422 pages, his most ambitious work until then. On the publisher's blog, there was no lack of anticipation about the importance of this book that Galera had waited four years to write, and about the new international exposure that its release promised to guarantee the author and the publisher, obviously.

From the beginning of the novel, which had been previously published as an excerpt in *Granta* magazine's selection of the 20 best young Brazilian writers, it becomes clear that the plot is captivating. The story's young protagonist, a triathlete who graduated in physical education and worked as a swimming teacher in Porto Alegre, has a revealing encounter with his father right before his suicide. Upset, he promises to kill his dog Beta, and he listens with interest to his father's account of his grandfather, a strong man with violent and contradictory passions who after becoming a widower fought for a fishermen's village in the state of Santa Catarina, where he disappeared apparently assassinated by the community in a primitive act of collective sacrifice for being an intruder. The narrator's story thereby develops in parallel with the grandfather's story. He adopts his father's dog and travels to Garopaba, on the coast of Santa Catarina, where he settles in an apartment on the beach and gets a job at a local gym while he looks for information about his grandfather's mysterious disappearance, a matter that was still sensitive and dangerous in the small town. There is, in this sense, a strong plot in the narrative that skillfully captivates the reader and that proceeds unexpectedly to a very surprising outcome, which will not be revealed here.

This narrative capacity was also evident in his previous novels, for example, in *The Shape of Bones*, in which a trip by the narrator to climb Cerro Bonete in Bolivia, in a sort of escape from everyday banality, suddenly unfolds into a trip to the past in search of a violent event that determined his development and adult life. Rustic, strong and enigmatic *gauchos* from the south of Brazil, with affective difficulties despite being very popular with women, are Galera's preferred heroes. Even in *Cordilheira*, in which the main character is Anita, a young Brazilian writer in Buenos Aires, the story focuses on the local character with whom she falls in love and who introduces her to a secret cult of writers. But the reader will likely not stop sympathizing with the character who, driven by intransigent principles and bordering on psychopathology, moves toward the extremes promised by the gradual escalation of the story with the ease of a detective plot.

In the beginning of the novel, the author places a metaliterary reference to "The South," the short story by Jorge Luis Borges about a man from the capital who, on a trip to the pampas and apparently trapped by an enigmatic call of destiny, becomes involved in a fatal knife duel. Galera's novel manages to guard its own secret, not falling into the temptation of tying all the loose ends of the outcome, and thus saves itself from the banality concealed by detectivist plots. But its quality goes beyond this. It is not a page-turner per se, full of action that guarantees the progression through short chapters with appealing hooks. The story progresses in a delightful ease of rhythm without letting go of a particular density in the raw material of the story, which seduces not only through the detailed descriptions but also through the convincing motivation of minute aspects in the narrative construction of the environments. Galera creates a peculiar and sensible realism through a density that manages to yield to the everyday described without atrophying the account and without descriptive excess. It is a kind of "intimate realism" in which the intimacy does not come from the protagonist's feelings or psychic meditations and interior dialogues, but from the descriptive precision of the chosen settings. Galera employs, here, a great device by inventing a neurological disease (prosopagnosia, or face blindness) for the character that keeps him from recognizing the facial features of other people and even himself. A certain ellipsis in the narrative is thus created in which the character's relative blindness is contrasted with the clearness of the described environments. One does not really know with whom he interacts, and a certain threat is established through the difficulty in interpreting the gestures of others. The invisible is introduced in the visible without abandoning descriptive transparency, and introduces in it an ambiguity that corroborates with the atmosphere of tension in the story's unfolding.

One easily sees the literary proximity of Galera to the contemporary Anglophone narrative, which is certainly a reference for the author. As a translator, Galera has worked with modern classics such as John Cheever, Hunter S. Thompson and Robert Crump, and he also translated the current voices of Zadie Smith, Jonathan Safran Foer and Irvine Welsh. But it is in Paul Auster's novels that characters such as this one are found: a man of our time who, catapulted by a crisis (his father's suicide, his brother's betrayal, his separation from his beloved wife), is led to seek explanations in a labyrinth of not always decipherable events. What is interesting in Galera's narrative is his capacity to create a convincing view of Brazilian reality without any vestiges of the eternal retrievals of a historical or cultural identity, and without picturesque and exotic temptations. The action takes place in the south, in Santa Catarina, and without a doubt in a contemporary context with clear historical characteristics and quickly identifiable social and cultural conflicts. It is premature to judge whether the plot manages to reflect the complexity of this situation, or whether the novel is up to its time. It is definitely a good story and an excellent novel. Will it be the novel of the decade and of its generation? Perhaps not.

Chapter 5

THE VICTORIOUS RETURN OF THE SELF IN CONTEMPORARY WRITING*

Despite the lack of precise statistical data, one of the most consistent features of contemporary narrative is the confident return of the first-person narrator. In recent novels, the first-person narrator reenters the scene without necessarily discussing its own condition of possibility, either in melancholic and solemn tones—such as, for example, in *Resistance*, by Julián Fuks—or in ironic and cynical tones—such as in *Brochadas* (Impotence), by Jacques Fux. The self has gained a new authority and resourcefulness through the testimony of its particular experience, or through the process that the writing reflects in its subjective formation. Thus, the position of the self reconciles an individual and his or her story by counting on a subjectivity in formation, and has thus gained a certain legitimacy. It is true that the central presence of the self is shared by a variety of genres that are not necessarily fictional, such as personal diaries, testimonies, self-help books, autobiographies, essays, memoirs, travel writing and everyday chronicles, among others, and that one of the explanations for this phenomenon probably resides in the approximation between the contemporary novel and these formats, which provokes a typical negotiation between reality and fiction. In the novel *The Eternal Son*, by Cristóvão Tezza, there is a good example in which fiction skillfully seams elements of memory discourses, self-help and confessional statements. The novel has come to earn great attention from the media, in addition to being a critical and commercial success as a result of this hybridity with very real foundations.

The concept of autofiction was coined from the debates on the diversity of the autobiographical genre in order to describe autobiographical narratives with great fictional freedom or fiction supported by biographical and referential elements from the life of the author. The introduction of biographical elements in these accounts, from real proper names to saucy or vengeful

---

* A previous version was published as "A volta vitoriosa do eu na narrativa contemporânea" in Maria Rosa Duarte; Maria José Palo. *Impasses do narrador e da narrativa*.

details of love affairs, without a doubt appeals to a public that wants to enjoy in literature not only the craftsmanship of language, but in particular the narcissistic celebrity of the writer, which has become an essential dimension of the publishing industry today. Thus, the author has resuscitated in literature and has installed himself or herself once again at the center of the narrative, with a precise and at times onomastic identification among author, narrator and character.

Ever since modernism, literature has nurtured a certain distrust in relation to the self as an enunciative authority. Rimbaud expressed this with precision in the celebrated phrase "I is an other" ("Je est un autre"), which became a warning against the illusions of a complete subjectivity. With the exception of the specific genres that were supported by subjective accounts, such as the autobiography, the travel account and the memoir, among others, the narrative self fell into disuse in detriment to a third-person neutrality. The literary theorist Wayne C. Booth (1961) characterized this distrust with his concept of the unreliable narrator, who is mainly in the first person. Modernity distanced itself from the exaltation of the lyrical self of romantic subjectivism and sought the neutrality of the third person as an alternative to the naiveness of a narrative self that was sincere and confident of its control over the effect of its own words. Maurice Blanchot underlined, in 1955, a fragment of Kafka's diary in which the young author comments on the "liberating passage from the first to the third person, from observation of oneself, which was Kafka's torment, to a higher observation, rising above mortal reality toward the other world, the world of freedom" (Blanchot 1982, 72). The benefit of this distancing in relation to the self was considered an "observation which has become act," converting literature into a force that wards off the oppression of the world. The neutrality and impersonality of the third person became the basis for the concept of writing that marked the understanding of modernist literature and the relation between expressive experimentation and the political dimension of its referentiality.

In contemporary literature the phenomenon of "autofiction" has been linked with a new legitimacy of the first-person pronoun "I" as an anchor for testimonial truth of individual experience. What is under discussion today is how writing can be seen in contemporaneity not just as a gesture of individual inscription and signature but also as a construction of pseudonimic secrecy as part of a performative insertion in representation. This type of *documentality*—equivalent to writing diary entries, annotations, opinions in social media and so on—sustains the social reality of individual acts and events and has often been analyzed from the perspective of memory and identity studies. As part of the argument we must consider the temporality of these interventions in the light of *presentification*: the effort to create an experience of simultaneity where the act of writing becomes part of the emergence of reality belonging both to its representation and to how representation affects social experience.

In 2011, many inhabitants of Rio de Janeiro became aware of the appearance of new inscriptions in the urban landscape by means of consistent and recognizable signs or letters from a mysterious and unknown alphabet. Intrigued by the enigmatic consistency of the writing, two mathematics students used a cryptographic algorithm to decipher the real content of the sentences collected all over the south side of the city. It turned out that the author was a 37-year-old woman, Joana César, who invented this secret alphabet when she was 12 years old and needed to protect her most intimate diary writings. As a grown-up, she revealed to the press, once identified by the mathematicians, that she felt compelled to register this exact content of her adolescent fantasies in public places such as tunnels, bridges or walls. Many compared the young artist to the famous "Profeta Gentileza"—*The Kindness Prophet*—a truck driver who received a vision after the circus disaster that occurred in Niteroi in 1961, when the Great North American Circus caught fire and was reduced to ashes, leaving a toll of over five hundred dead, most of them children. After this terrible disaster, José Datrino (known as prophet Gentileza), then 44 years old, started to dedicate his life to leaving inscriptions of moral content in public spaces in Rio de Janeiro, the most famous of these being the phrase *Gentileza gera Gentileza* ("Kindness creates kindness"). By his death in 1996, Gentileza was a widely known personality in Rio de Janeiro and many of his writings were protected and preserved by the municipality.

In the cases of Joana César and Gentileza but also in the random signatures of the common Brazilian *pichadores*, graffiti activists normally not considered as artists, we are dealing with interventions in the public space motivated by personal or intimate intentions but with political, ethical or aesthetic consequences. Here we see a kind of *documentality*, in the sense used by Maurizio Ferraris,[1] as opposed to John Searle's concept of *intentionality* and in the attempt to offer a realistic notion of *social object* and—as such—a key category of social ontology. Writing is stronger than speech, argues Ferraris, and for the Italian philosopher the concept of *documentality* maintains that the construction of social objects is to be found in the "act of recording" and is rooted both in the theory of *performatives* and *speech acts*[2] and the theory of *inscription*.[3]

The act of recording is divided into three hierarchical levels of writing capable of bringing thought into the world. Ferraris distinguishes between

---

[1] Maurizio Ferraris (2012).
[2] Austin (1962).
[3] Derrida ([1967] 2016).

trace, register and *inscription*, where trace is a simple intervention on the surface, an index that permits us to recall something absent. Register is the representation of this record in our mind, whereas the inscription is the external exhibition of this representation, which is what gives it social value and converts it into a "common object" for collective access. On the one hand, Ferraris makes a distance to constructivism and the spiritual power of creating reality through language, underlining the institutional necessity of written documents to enable subjective intentions to become reality; on the other hand, he weakens the theory of inscription summarized in the famous Derrida phrase: "There is nothing outside the text." In Ferraris's realistic version the sentence becomes "There is nothing *social* outside the text." Beyond the social reality, Ferraris recognizes *Natural objects*, which exist in space and time independent of subjects, and *Ideal objects*, which exist outside space and time independent of subjects, both of which are very different from *Social objects*, whose existence in space and time depend on subjects. So it is only for social objects that the theory of *documentality* becomes important, in obedience to the equation "*Object = Inscribed Act.*"

Following this idea, the previous examples must be considered on one hand as social objects created out of personal and often intimate inscription of traces on the surface of urban experience. On the other hand, it is easy to recognize that this documentation does not serve as a stable ground for *institutions* but rather strives to *underwrite* the relationship to already stable institutions through strategies of secrecy, irony and antagonicity. In the case of the Brazilian "*pichadores*," the example worth citing is the *São Paulo Biennial* of 2008, where a part of the space reserved for the biennial activities were kept empty by the organizers for the purpose of discussing the curatorial challenges of contemporary art; perhaps not surprisingly, this area was invaded by 40 *pichadores* who left their marks on the white walls of the exhibition palace in *Ibirapuera Park*. A young girl, Caroline Pivetta, was caught and spent 54 days incarcerated for vandalism. In 2010, the biennial organizers invited the same *pichadores* to participate in the exhibition with drawings and paintings instead of sprays. In the case of Joana César from Rio de Janeiro, the public disclosure of her secret diary exposed in cryptographic form in the public space of the city immediately put an end to her activities in the streets. The positive aspect of this fact is that she received invitations from art galleries and started a new career as a painter; though without ever recovering the force of her former activities in her attempts to recreate the visual expression of her wall inscriptions in large paintings.

If we turn to contemporary literature in this perspective, another question becomes relevant, namely, the status of subjectivity that obviously cannot only be understood as and reduced to "intentionality," this being the main point of

Maurizio Ferraris's criticism of John Searle's theory of *Social Reality*. Subjects are also "objects" of the desire and the acts of others and can become social images through media representation or other forms of biographical construction and exposure. In the case of the writing subject, the subject of documentation, the effect of writing is not only transitive but also intransitive, as stressed in the well-known essay by Roland Barthes,[4] with its transformative power over authorial subjectivity. We will discuss this later but now let us just take a sample of the contemporary Brazilian narrative in which a recovered legitimacy of first-person narratives, a certain preference for what has been coined *autofiction*, has been recognized by critics. Choosing three novels from 2016, we can reach a closer understanding of what this return to a certain confessional or testimonial narrative might mean: *Descobri que estava morto* by João Paulo Cuenca, *A vista particular* by Ricardo Lísias and *Simpatia pelo Demônio* by Bernardo Carvalho. Very different proposals, different styles and narrative modes, yet all three with a similar construction: a fictional plot involving a main character based on the author's biographical experience and a historical background narrative closely linked to factual characters and recent political events. In the novel by João Paulo Cuenca, the narrator tells the story of "João Paulo Cuenca" in the first person and starts the narration with the sentence: "I discovered that I was dead when I tried to write a book. Still not *this* book." The recent past is in this way narrated from the writing present to gain an effect of *presentification*. It is as if we readers were following the narrations becoming present through our experience of reading simultaneously with the writing present. The narrator discovers that in 2011 a person was found dead in possession of the narrator's (and the author's) personal documents, in an abandoned building occupied by homeless squatters in the neighborhood of Lapa in Rio de Janeiro. He starts to investigate this enigmatic fact and the puzzling evidence he discovers points to a fatal outcome: the writer ends up killed. On the one hand, an obviously contrafactual ending to our knowing that the author survived, together with the alluring exploitation of accurate biographical details culled from the real life of the writer. At the same time, we are presented with a close and critical account of the large-scale urban reforms ahead of the big events of the 2014 World Cup, the 2016 Olympic Games, and now a huge corruption scheme that has landed the state governor and his close collaborators in prison. Parts of the city were gentrified, the slums were kept under close surveillance to improve security during the events, and entire neighborhoods were removed to facilitate building the Olympic facilities. Also in the novel by Ricardo Lísias, contextual events are narrated

---

[4] Roland Barthes, 'To Write: An Intransitive Verb?' [1966], *The Rustle of Language* (1986).

with documental precision and described with geographical and temporal accuracy. The narrative format resembles a multimedia script comparable to a story board. In spite of the ironic development of the fictional plot, the novel registers almost real-time events and characters; this likens the writing to the day-to-day intervention of a newspaper chronicle. It could also be compared to the temporality of registers written in social media, which in turn are simultaneous with representation of historical events through the media. Again this strategy of writing could be considered a search for "presentification," this being understood both as claiming a temporality of immediacy and creating effects of sensible presence. The first dimension is observed in the immediacy of the creative process itself, compromised by its content, while the second is expressed as a challenge to intervene in the actuality of a complex social and political present. We observe how the distance between creation and reception is shortened by technological platforms: the writer is online and the experience of this temporality zero accentuates the performatic aspect of his or her endeavor. The book is still the main vehicle of contemporary literature but the writing of the book is part of its content, not as a modern meta-literary reflection on the power of fiction but as an appropriation of the reality targeted by its inscription. The writer today is committed to registering his own creation in real-time, publicly reflecting the creative process and interacting with a network of daily-life contingencies. A peculiar kind of *self-writing*, a theatrical staging of the creative process, an ethnographic register that accompanies the constellation of information and representation in which it is being inscribed and where the clear limits between fiction and reality becomes blurred. Fiction gains reality and the reality of fiction changes status becoming not a "historical reality" but the lived experience of "daily-life reality" in zero-time, submitted neither to space nor to the difference between "close" and "distant," local and global in a historical time where dreams and fantasies are explored and expropriated by technological media. Fiction finds its challenge in exploring the conversion of certain images into reality, thus underlining its performative and affective dimension. Instead of a distinct public sphere, the separation between the individual, the social and public imagination deprivatizes privacy and openly expresses the private experience.

The literary documentation of the present projects a virtual temporality that blends facts of presence end events of imagination with a reality that becomes prophetic or at least points to emergency as if it were a memory of a present open to what has happened, what is happening and what will eventually happen.

But what are the actual conditions for the success of such an investment in the reality of literary writing? We are obviously far beyond the modern ambitions of representative realism so often restaged during the twentieth century in diverse forms of new realism. The stakes for this kind of writing challenge the very autonomy of literature in its search for intervention in the effective reality of a circumstantial world. Josefina Ludmer polemically denominates this interdependency as postautonomous writing willing to suspend the question of the aesthetic value of its endeavor and submit to the determination of reality. As such, writing becomes the suspension of the difference between subject and object and the involuntary bearer of an experience without a subject, which is very close to what Roland Barthes characterized as the "intransitive writing" of modernism in his 1966 essay "To Write: An Intransitive Verb?"[5] The writer writes but is at the same time "written," a phenomenon described as *Diathesis*, which Barthes claims "designates the way in which the subject of the verb is affected by the action. This is obvious for the passive; and yet linguists tell us that, in Indo-European at least, the diathetical opposition is not between active and passive but between active and middle." (Barthes, 11) Barthes refers here to the famous 1950 essay by Benveniste,[6] "Active and Middle Voice in the Verb," on the existence of a "middle voice," neither active nor passive, as in the verb *sacrifice* in Sanskrit, where he notes a difference between the verb when speaking about the sacrifice of another and when dealing with self-sacrifice. Barthes observes that "the middle voice corresponds exactly to the modern state of the verb *to write*: to write is today to make oneself the center of the action of speech, it is to effect writing by affecting oneself, to make action and affection coincide, to leave the *scriptor* inside the writing—not as a psychological subject (the Indo-European priest could perfectly well be overflowing with subjectivity while actively sacrificing for his client)—but as agent of the action" (18). It is well-known how this essay had a strong influence on the early structuralists and Jacques Derrida, who invoked it in 1968 in his essay on *Différance*, a concept identified as an operation "*that cannot be conceived either as passion or as the action of a subject on an object.*"[7] For Derrida, the middle voice represented a certain intransitive state of thought or philosophy that only through repression was constituted as active or passive.

Modernism expressed this critical view of the subject of writing as a romantic entity prior to its expression. In modernism the theory of the expressive writing subject was constituted, according to Barthes, by a subjectivity "immediately contemporary with the writing, being effected and affected by it." This would be the exemplary case of the Proustian narrator who exists only by writing. Underlying this vision, modernism embraced a libertarian

---

[5] "To Write: An Intransitive Verb?" [1966], in Barthes (1986, 11–21).
[6] "Active and Middle Voice in the Verb" [1950], in Benveniste ([1966] 1973, 145–51).
[7] Derrida ([1972] 1982, 9).

ideal of a transgression of the subject-object distinction, thereby enabling access to what Benjamin called an "absolute experience."

The radicalness of this affirmation arguably consists in reformulating the question of referentiality for modern literature, letting go of a model of representability supported by the ontology of the subject/object relation and abandoning with it the instance of "reality" as exterior to writing. By insisting on the creation of literature in this manner, Barthes criticizes an aesthetics of art for art's sake, vindicating work with "form" in a more radical way as "the only possible space of *the one who writes*" (Barthes 1986, 20), to the extent that it is here that referentiality itself reappears in its affective dimension. In modern languages, the middle voice no longer has its own place, but has left its reflexive forms. However, other experiments in writing have arisen that discursively create the same ambiguity between active and passive, such as, for example, free indirect discourse—*erlebte Rede*—in clear enunciative positions. Thus, direct and indirect discourse, first and third person, author and narrator, narrator and character end up being effaced, leaving a more complex and more concrete reading experience that negotiates the clear boundaries between the subject and object of speech.

Contrary to the critics who accuse the writers of high modernism of a frivolous and aestheticizing use of language, Barthes shows a political and ethical commitment in his theory of modern writing that precipitates contemporary discussions on the affective dimension of literature, as well as the view of the performative character of writing, which is manifest in the affective dimension of the reality encompassed. Such a theory brings referentiality to the heart of writing and simultaneously makes evident the effect on the subject who writes in a constitutive way of the subjectivity that is here expressed. It is in this theoretical milestone that it becomes possible to situate properly the idea of writing as an aesthetics of existence and of literature as a self-writing, since one recognizes the performance of writing in the affective incorporation of the object and as a subjectifying power over whoever writes.

"I am a sick man," begins the narrator in Dostoyevsky's *Notes from the Underground*, and a first-person discourse follows that is always marked by a fissure, a lack, an anomaly. Curiously enough, this is how the impersonal and anonymous element appears in the self and how we recognize it in João Gilberto Noll's narrators and more recently in, for example, *Divórcio* (Divorce) and *O céu dos suicidas* (Suicide sky), by Ricardo Lísias. Here, the first person seems to deepen the flaw of a hurt subject, who is characterized by anesthesia or alienation in the face of an all-too-present reality, or, as in Noll, by an affective weakness that traumatically aggravates the narrator's bodily condition. Today, this is not the customary path for authors who employ their personal and autobiographical experiences to build the narrative. In some cases, personal experience seems to take the place of the historical dimension of the modern novel, though in cases such as that of *Nowhere People*, by Paulo Scott, the autobiographical aspect ends up bringing an allegorical perspective to the disillusioned interpretation of recent Brazilian history, which approximates the novel to traditional coming-of-age (*Bildung*) formats. In the novels *Diary of the Fall* and *Poison Apple*, by Michel Laub, the reference to the author's life is always explicit and (intentionally?) calls for interpretations that identify the narratives with the author's experiences. Silviano Santiago plays with format in *Histórias mal contadas* (Badly told stories) and *O falso mentiroso* (The fake liar), but always in tune with an elliptic deconstruction of the protagonist's individual identity. In *Spilt Milk*, by Chico Buarque de Hollanda, the view of the self offers the narrative possibility of expressing a mind diluted by dementia, a paradox in a time obsessed by the preservation of memory. In *Pornopopeia*, by Reinaldo Morais, and *Brochadas* (Impotence), by Jacques Fux, the slapstick humor saves a self that is almost hyperbolic in its self-confidence and, via Rabelaisian irony, creates a healthy distance from the dangers of an overly confident masculinity. In the recent novel *A realidade devia ser proibida* (Reality should be prohibited), by Maria Clara Drummond, the author, due to the absence of this distance in her story, misses a great opportunity to create a really interesting portrait of the futility of the Brazilian elite, as the American Bret Easton Ellis was able to do in corrosive fashion in the novels *American Psycho* and *Less Than Zero*, or as Nicholson Baker does in the ever satirically confessional speech of *Vox* and *Fermata*.

The return of the identification among author, narrator and character occurs in a huge variety of approaches and styles, some of them clearing pioneering paths for contemporary literature, such as the melancholic essayism of Sebald in *The Rings of Saturn*, the narrative elegance of Bruce Chatwin in *What Am I Doing Here*, or the corrosive resentment of Thomas Bernhard in *Gathering Evidence*, not to mention the expository radicalness of *My Struggle*, by Karl Knausgaard. It is impossible to offer an analysis that encompasses all this variety, but the argument here understands the phenomenon based on the perspective of the general tendency of a growing demand for the real that guides a large part of the media, cultural and artistic products of contemporaneity. We are flooded by "realities" represented by the media in real time, and our own identity is more and more dependent on its circulation in this social media sphere, in which the real is hardly distinguishable from the fictional.

To bring elements of one's own life to the story is not only difficult to avoid, but also intentional in these cases, because it sparks interest among readers and spectators. In the seminal text by Josefina Ludmer on postautonomous literatures, the argument is that the contemporary has conditioned a writing that is very different from the "modernist writing" of Roland Barthes and that can no longer be read with the literary expectation of formal and aesthetic experimentation, nor properly as representations of the writer's reality. Its realism is not in the representation, but rather in the capacity to "manufacture a present" via direct testimony, which is not compromised by the exactness of its recording, but primarily by the presence that it seeks to produce without considering the boundaries between reality and fiction, between personal experience and the reality created by the media, by technology and by science. This testimony's proper environment is the everyday, Ludmer says, which is characterized by a reality that does not want to be represented because it is already pure representation: a texture of words and images of different velocities, degrees, and densities that are inside/outside a subject, which not only includes the event, but also the virtual, the potential, the magical, and the fantasmatic (Ludmer 2007). From this perspective of a "public imagination" or "factory of the present," in which literary and artistic production is necessarily situated and traditional hermeneutics fails for lack of sense and depth, the differences between reality and fiction, between author and character, are effaced. In Ludmer's view, we are living in a sort of pathologized public sphere in which the relation between public and private is inverted, thus exhibiting intimacy for public enjoyment at the same time that politics—as well as power and the economy—is determined in more and more private circles.

The fascination for the exposure of large and small disasters and atrocities pathologizes the public sphere with regard to traumatic wounds via a suffering that somehow becomes collective, for it unites and emotionally involves everyone. An ambiguity arises that threatens the solid boundaries between collective forms of representation, exposure, testimony and the singularity or privacy of the subject, which is expressed in the confusion between the psychic and the social, between the outside—the world—and the inside—the self. As a consequence of this pathology, a certain traumatophilia arises in the media and in art, in which the narrative structure of trauma gains in popularity and becomes a banalized heuristic figure for the relation to the past, in which false testimony is converted into a clue for the therapeutic recognition of history. The pathology of the public sphere sows the suspicion that we are all victims of a past wound that authorizes our story and legitimizes its testimony.

As emphasized by Ludmer, the format that is confirmed in the contemporary is the testimony of the everyday chronicle, in which one constructs the account both of notable events and of the ephemeral based on the perspective of one's own experience. The referentiality of the account does not distinguish what is real from what is fantasy, but the experience witnessed is made present in this staging of the subject, which thus seems to give some meaning to existence, and in relation to which confessional intimism acquires new authority. With the return of the private universe, traditional confessionalism resuscitates with a new legitimacy by exploring the (auto)biographical differential that defines the individual to the extent that he or she is converted into a testimony of his or her particular condition. From this perspective, a discussion on the differences in genre between autobiography and autofiction is no longer relevant, since the question of referentiality is absorbed by the performativity of testimony itself and its effects of presence.

Rancière points out the break in the pact "between the impersonality of art and that of its material" as a result of a renewed role of authorial ownership in the contemporary (Rancière 2010, 104). Never before has the author been such an owner, not so much of his or her style and work, but of the idea that he or she exerts and of the actual image that he or she produces. "The author *par excellence* is supposedly the one who exploits what already belongs to him, his own image. The author is then no longer the 'spiritual histrion' of which Mallarmé spoke, but the comedian of his image" (Rancière 2010, 105). But is there, in the construction of this autofictional image, some legitimacy that one could understand in light of the Foucaultian idea of a self-writing, of an aesthetics of existence? The question that needs to be asked is whether or not literature is the right place for a more radical demand for truth. It is clear that "truth" is not meant here in a naïve sense. Testimony must however assume that which Foucault, in his final courses, discussed with respect to the notion of parrhesia (i.e., frankness, sincerity), to speak the truth even if it puts one's own life at risk. The truth does not refer to the ontology of the word, but to the empathic sincerity of the subject that is performative as self-writing, not as a result of a fictional freedom of autobiographical restaging, as in works by Sophie Calle, or, in another manner, by Cindy Sherman, but as a risky wager that carries palpable consequences. The introduction of autobiographical elements, of biographemes, constitutes an element of extralinguistic contingency that tends to impact discourse with a deixis effect that compromises the discursive subject in another way.

In order to distinguish the subject of enunciation from the grammatical subject of the statement, or the author from the narrator, Foucault introduces the category of *enunciandum* ("enunciating"), which refers to the belief or opinion of the speaker.[8] What is interesting about the study of this notion in Foucault, which comes from the domain of *bios*, that is, from the subject's life experience, is that, in parrhesia, the speaker underscores the fact that he is, at the same time, the subject of the enunciation and the subject of the statement, that he himself is of the opinion to which he refers. To be sincere means to say: I am the one who thinks this or that, and furthermore, I am willing to run

---

[8] See Foucault (1999).

the risk implicit in this truth—which is mine—even if it places my own life on the line. We thus perceive that art and life are somehow tied together again, contrary to the modern characteristics that Rancière (2011) defines in the perspective of an aesthetic regime of art.

With the definition of art as its own sphere of experience, with the autonomy of literature, the ties to other forms of sensible experience are cut, and this separation between art and life is one of the defining characteristics of the aesthetic regime. Postautonomy, for its part, brings back characteristics similar to those of the ethical regime, which is defined in the scope of the Platonic theory of the image. In the production that is anchored in autobiographical elements, art and life are once again inseparable. It does not occur due to a hierarchy of ontological values that, in the classical era, defined the appropriateness of a certain genre (tragedy, for elevated themes, and comedy, for lower ones) for ethically defined contents, nor due to the rules of rhetoric. The ethical dimension appears in the contemporary due to the singular value that the subject of enunciation, the author, gives to the reality expressed and to how he or she appears through it. The reality effect, its "realism," thus depends on this connection and on the force of and eventual interest in his or her autofiction as an aesthetics of existence, also. If the autobiographical account wants to gain some relevance, in the face of the general frivolity of the cult of celebrity, and if literature still intends to assume the critical role of "free speech," it must submit to this critical filter, which is explained in exemplary fashion by Leiris:

> To reject all fable, to admit as materials only actual facts (and not only probable facts, as in the classical novel), nothing but these facts and all these facts, was the rule I had imposed upon myself. Already a trail had been blazed for me by André Breton's *Nadja*, but I dreamed above all of making my own that project Baudelaire was inspired to undertake after reading a passage in Poe's *Marginalia*: to lay bare one's heart, to write that book about oneself in which the concern for sincerity would be carried to such lengths that, under the author's sentences, "the paper would shrivel and flare at each touch of his fiery pen." (1984, 158)

The destiny of modernity and the society of spectacle, in Giorgio Agamben's apocalyptic vision, is massive alienation. Even so, Agamben recognizes a libertarian potential in the emptiness provoked by alienation, an experience of language itself. The reversal of alienation can happen in the authorial gesture because according to his reading of Foucault's essay "What is an author," subjectivity must be seen as gesture. While Foucault considered writing not as much "the expression of the subject as the opening of a space in which the writing subject does not cease to disappear" (61), for Agamben this disappearance is a dynamic potency, and subjectivity is in a way measured by its similarity to authorship. This surprisingly optimistic view of the existential emptiness of contemporaneity is hard to maintain when looking into real-life examples where the search for individual affirmation, rather than vanity, seems to express despair. If contemporary writers in Latin America reinvent in fiction their own biographical content as prime material, it is not out of a new "romantic" confidence in the self and the truth of lived experience and its intimate expression, but rather much more a recognition of subjectivity as an approach to connectivity, as a biopolitical bundle in time and space that can be renegotiated in fiction and become a lens of interpretation or even a focal point for global comprehension. This is what we could see in the former mentioned novels by Cuenca and Lísias, and it happens in Bernardo Carvalho's novel *Simpatia pelo Demônio* (Sympathy for the devil), where the main character, the UN employee and expert in violence studies who is sent on a mission to rescue a person kidnapped by ISIS or some such organization, only gets to understand violence and submission intimately through a homo-erotic relationship described, even in a third-person narrative, based on evident biographical and confessional life experience.

Another aspect must be taken into account in order to understand this apparition of the "author" figure in the world of fiction, an aspect that cannot be understood only in terms of the narcissism inherent to media culture. One must consider the fact that the boundaries between reality and fiction are constantly being challenged, not simply because historical experience turns into fiction through real-time coverage of events, but also because the literary and artistic seek political insertion in reality. Writers and artists yearn to appear, intervene and change the reality of things not for the sake of the critical precision of their aesthetic representation or expression. No, what they really want is for literary or artistic creation itself to adopt a different attitude, so much so that creation becomes the real pivot of this longing. This is a bit more visible in contemporary art, seeing that artists either *perform* their art, or introduce politics as a theme and object, or else adopt a position outside the restrained milieus of museums and galleries to relate to communities, groups, individuals, and political matters.

The relational and performatic aspect emerges as a feature that helps to define contemporary art. In the case of literature, and above all in fiction, the performatic factor is less literal and more connected to the linguistic question of acts of speech and deictic referentiality, if always in a less direct fashion. Ricardo Lísias is an exception in that his fictional production has reflected in real and legal life in a manner both rather undesirable—when he was sued for criminal misrepresentation on the grounds of a legal document that he recreated in his novel "*Divórcio*" (Divorce)—and at the same time desired—when he used the same experience in "*Delegado Tobias*" (Sheriff Tobias) or edited a narrative on the time that the corrupt politician Eduardo Cunha spent in jail ("*Diário da Cadeia*" (Jail Diary), which he signed using Cunha's name as a pseudonym. Without dwelling on the phenomenon of "self-fiction," We would suggest that the increasingly frequent appearance of the author's figure—sometimes dressed "self-fictionally"—should be seen as a symptom of a more fundamental transformation that affects the very autonomy that characterized modern art and literature, a change that insinuates relinquishing aesthetic hegemony. The Russian art historian and critic, Boris Groys, has remarked that the *contemporary* is characterized by a shift from the contemplative attitude that makes an aesthetic judgment of the work—an attitude that predominates modern aesthetics—to a position of art production that stresses the technical and poetic aspects of *performing* art. Today's public is more interested in producing than just observing the image. With the proliferation of the Internet's platforms of worldwide digital communication, allied with easy access to cell phones with cameras, art production now extends beyond aesthetic contemplation. At the same time, this image is primarily the image of whoever produces it, in other words, what becomes the principal object is the produced image of the subject's aesthetic expression.

We are all called to assume the authorship of ourselves, to design our own appearance, image, or aesthetic form for the general contemplation of the public. This "generalized authorship" is part of another fundamental shift in the role of arts and literature in the contemporary world, and once again Groys helps us to describe it as moving from the aesthetic to the poetic, from the contemplative paradigm that determines modern art since Kant's third criticism, to a question of poiesis, that is to say, a technical question of the production of the work, just as it was necessary for the poetics of Aristotle. If the aesthetic attitude emerged to the detriment of poetics quite recently, Groys suggests that now it is time to re-focus on the poetic aspect by analyzing the probability of artistic production. This happens at the peak of vanguard art when Duchamp's gesture led to the artistic object losing its importance to the perspective of "performing" or the artistic gesture that at the same time sponsors the artist himself as an objective of art. In contemporary art, works are presented as the incarnation of a subjectivity without any specific content.

The Argentine critic Reinaldo Laddaga observes that contemporary literature covets the same condition as contemporary visual arts, converts narrative into an interactive route stimulated by a contingent set of scenarios that constantly questions the relation between production and reception, and joins *reading* to the collective realization that tends to expose individual, aesthetic contemplation to its power as an ethical and communitarian gift. If literary modernity symbolically stressed reading rather than the productive creativity of writing (Pierre Menard), the contemporary seems to prefer another view of writing as no longer being a privilege of the chosen few but rather the interactive media *par excellence* that negotiates new frontiers between subjective construction and participating in the general appropriating of what is already written as a way of interacting with the collective.

Chapter 6

CRITICISM FROM THE PERIPHERY— FOR ANOTHER MISPLACED IDEA*

> Politics arises *between* men, and so quite *outside* of man. There is therefore no real political substance. Politics arises in what lies *between men* and is established as relationships […] politics organizes those who are absolutely different with a view to their *relative* equality and in contradistinction to their *relative* differences.
>
> Hannah Arendt[1]

The relation between center and periphery is an epistemological question that guides a large part of historical discussions in Brazilian criticism and establishes the understanding of national characteristics in opposition to the hegemonic tendencies coming from the outside, namely from Europe and the United States, in particular. It is impossible to understand the discussions around the national question in literature and art since independence without considering this comparative mirror, a necessary condition for identifying differences and recognizing similarities among Brazilian authors and their influences from international canonical models, or from an effectively existing world literature (*Weltliteratur*). It is clear that the aforementioned relation is not established only among books, that behind it there is the structure of the publishing industry whose expansion introduced literary forms and themes mainly in the novel's attainment of hegemony, as Franco Moretti demonstrated in his famous study of the geography of the nineteenth-century novel (*Atlas of the European Novel*).

What would be the role, then, if any, of literature produced in Brazil in relation to a *Weltliteratur*, which Goethe considered to be the necessary future

---

* A previous version of this chapter was published as "A literatura brasileira contemporânea na perspectiva mundial" in *Literatura e Artes na Crítica Contemporânea*.
[1] See Arendt (2005, 95–96).

and destiny of German literature? Today, the field of world literature is successfully emerging as an unprecedented success and becoming the lifesaver for the main university programs of comparative literature. In one of his pioneering works on the theme, "Conjectures on World Literature" (2000), the critic Franco Moretti tries to model a theory on the world expansion of the European novel that is inspired by Darwinian evolutionism and by Immanuel Wallerstein's world-systems theory and economic history. Moretti thinks of world literature in parallel to world capitalism as a system that is both "one" and "unequal," and which developed in the expansion of the center to the periphery. By dominating or subjugating and even eliminating traditional genres and forms, such a system thus accompanies the political and economic development of colonization and neocolonization by creating roots in cultures with less history and tradition, on the one hand, and inspiring creativity, on the other, but only after overcoming the first derivative resistances. Moretti's description ultimately does not correspond to the one system of world literature with interconnected literatures that Goethe and later Marx imagined, for its tendency is deeply unequal.

Faithful to the historical-materialist theoretical foundation, Moretti understands such an evolutionary process of expansion and development as imminently dialectical, and it is interesting for our discussion to highlight the inspiration that he encounters in Brazilian criticism, mainly in the theories of Roberto Schwarz, who in the essay "The Importing of the Novel to Brazil and Its Contradictions in the Work of Alencar," and in various other posterior works, analyzes national literature as *indebted* to European literature. This process of indebtedness, notice the economic metaphor, is deeply asymmetrical and develops in literature concomitantly with social and economic history, creating more and more inequality and emphasizing the superiority of the novel as the European form par excellence. It is easy to recognize Schwarz's critical vision of the nineteenth century Brazilian literature, and it is not strange that he of all people serves as an example for Moretti. "The modern novel," the critic writes, "first arises not as an autonomous development but as a compromise between a western formal influence (usually French or English) and local materials" (Moretti 2000). Thus, Moretti insists on the oneness of the literary system despite recognizing that it is a system of variations created by local materials and also by local forms, since he recognizes in Schwarz that a part of the original historical conditions reappears in the sociological form, the forms being abstract representations of specific social relations.

There is no need here to develop the criticisms made in the Brazilian context vis-à-vis Schwarz's theory of cultural dependency. However, one might note that it generated one of the main discussions that defined the critical environment during the 1960s, 1970s and 1980s. It is enough to remember scathing responses from Silviano Santiago, Haroldo de Campos and Luiz Costa Lima—for example, in the essay "Atração do Mundo" (Attraction of the World), by Silviano Santiago, which criticizes the eurocentrism of Joaquim Nabuco—to Antonio Candido, who reinforces in Brazil a consciousness of "underdevelopment" and "backwardness." As Eneida Maria de Souza observes, an oscillation is established, in the discussion around the "dialectical identity of Brazilian culture," between "the local and the universal, the same and the other, civilization and primitivism, the modern and the archaic." This oscillation is manifested "either through positive dialectics— Oswald de Andrade and the poetics of Pau-Brasil, the Tropicalism of the 1960s—or through negative dialectics—Machado de Assis and the lesson of the mismatch between capitalist modernity and the Brazilian experience" (Souza 2002, 49).[2] In Brazilian criticism, the first position is mainly defended by Silviano Santiago—"Latin American Discourse: The Space In-Between" (1972) and "Universality in Spite of Dependency" (1981)—and the second in the arguments by Roberto Schwarz from, for example, "Misplaced Ideas" (1992) and "Brazilian Culture: Nationalism by Elimination" (1988). The polemic develops forcefully as a vector for the landscape of Brazilian academic criticism and culminates around the modernist project of Oswald de Andrade and in the evaluation of the adequacy of anthropophagy, which constitutes for Santiago the real possibility of a strong and authentic nationality and for Schwarz the expression of a conservative-progressive myth. Years later, in 2002, in a speech prepared for the Frankfurt Fair, Silviano Santiago will criticize the condition of national culture from another perspective, in which he regrets the incapacity to adjust to the world panorama after the fall of the Berlin Wall. If the end of the Cold War transformed ideologically fossilized political values, it created in Brazil a "geological fault in the Brazilian scene," laying the ground for a writer such as Paulo Coelho to be transformed into a global representative of Brazilian literature.

By becoming small-minded, the Portuguese language reduced, for its part, the possibility of and capacity for any speaker to be adequately and critically included in the disturbed end-of-century reality. Everything happened among us as if the wall had fallen out there, far away from

---

[2] The original version in Portuguese reads: "identidade dialética da cultura brasileira [...] o local e o universal, o mesmo e o outro, a civilização e o primitivismo, o moderno e o arcaico [...] ora a través da dialética positiva-Oswald de Andrade e a poética de Pau-Brasil, o tropicalismo dos anos 1960—ora pela dialética negativa—Machado de Assis e a lição do descompasso entre a modernidade capitalista e a experiência brasileira."

Brazil, and its debris had not compromised the everyday behavior and reflexive speech of Brazilians ("Outubro Retalhado" [October in Shreds]).[3]

In the classic text "The National Instinct," published originally in 1873, Machado de Assis offers a well-known reading of this relation, which became a reference for any student and professor of Brazilian literature. Contrary to the excesses of the exalted Romanticism of Gonçalves Dias to Santa Rita Durão, Assis proposes that "What we should expect from the writer above all is a certain intimate feeling that renders him a man of his time and country, even when he addresses topics that are remote in time or space" (2018, 89). That is, the dialectical solution presented here is to find the universality of an intimate feeling even in "topics that are remote in time or space" (89). Here, one clearly sees how Assis places his confidence in finding a universality at the heart of the national dimension, which helps to transform the writer into a man of his "time." The national is converted into the universal as long as writers assume their stories, the particularities of their time, a time still marked by backwardness in comparison to "more developed literatures," to use Assis's own expression (92). It is nevertheless left to the critic to discover this Brazilian "intimate feeling," just as the French critic mentioned by Assis found a Scottishness in Masson that was "distinct and superior for not being merely superficial" (89). In other words, one articulates a confidence that the national characteristic exists more deeply in its distinctive features than can be identified on the surface—for example, in the descriptions of its natural settings, of its circumstantial reality and of its historical characteristics—by bringing to light its connection to a universal humanism. Nonetheless, in addition to the distinctive features, the contributions to Brazilian culture of Amerindian and African cultures, which are ignored on behalf of abstract human values, are also effaced. Strictly speaking, there was no absolute contrast between national values and the universal values of a cosmopolitanism that still seemed distant for a nineteenth-century Brazilian, despite being nourished by an Enlightenment hope, already articulated by Kant in 1794,[4] that the philosophical universality of Reason would somehow find its geopolitical realization in

---

[3] The original version in Portuguese reads: "falha geológica na cena brasileira [...] Ao se amesquinhar, a língua portuguesa reduziu, por sua vez, a possibilidade e a capacidade de qualquer falante de se inserir adequada e criticamente na realidade conturbada do final do século. Tudo se passou entre nós como se o muro tivesse caído lá fora, léguas daqui, e seus escombros não tivessem comprometido o comportamento cotidiano e a fala reflexiva dos brasileiros."

[4] See Kant (2008).

new institutions participating in the creation of an ethical-political totality of a world republic (*Weltrepublik*).

First, it becomes necessary to determine whether or not there is a hidden and exaggerated confidence, here, in the possibility of a dialectical overcoming of opposites, of the particular and the universal, of the national and the global and of Brazilian literature and world literature. Is it not this same confidence in dialectics that nourishes the thinking of, for example, Antonio Candido when he announces his faith "in the synthesis of particular and universal tendencies" (Santiago 1996, 32)?[5] Or when Schwarz, in the development of his sharp argument about "misplaced ideas" in nineteenth-century Brazil, still cries over backwardness, dependency and the lack of dialectical adequacy between the ideological and political inventory and the real development of modernization in Brazilian society? Let us recall that in Roberto Schwarz's analysis of Machado de Assis, this mismatch between capitalist modernity and capitalist experience is the raw material of the writer when he brings "into the foreground the modernization that came with Capital" in the ridiculous figure of the "Francophile or Germanophile," or of "the ideologies of progress, of liberalism, of reason" (Schwarz 1980, 46–47). Curiously enough, Schwarz disconsiders the critical potency of this mismatch, or in his words, this always "improper" repositioning of European ideas (47).[6]

For Machado de Assis, in the essay "The National Instinct," and for Roberto Schwarz in "Misplaced Ideas," the possibility of synthesis departed from nationalism or the national perspective in the direction of the outside world,[7] while for Joaquim Nabuco the perspective was inverted and assumed globalization as the fundamental premise: "I am more a spectator of my century than of my country. For me, the play is civilization, and it is staged in all the great theaters of humankind, now connected by the telegraph."[8] There is a marked difference here between a perspective from the inside out and a perspective from the outside in, despite the latter being a result of a Eurocentric

---

[5] The original version in Portuguese reads: "na síntese de tendências particularistas e universalistas."

[6] "In their quality of being improper, they will be material and a problem for literature. The writer may well not know this, nor does he need to, in order to use them. But he will be off-key unless he feels, notes, and develops—or wholly avoids—this aspect" (Schwarz 1980, 47).

[7] "And for one more variation of the same theme, let us conclude by saying that even when dealing with the most modest matters of everyday life, the subject matter of our novelists has always been world-historical. This they shaped as well as they could, but it would not have been their subject, had they dealt with it directly" (Schwarz 1980, 49).

[8] Quoted in Jackson (2008, 341–42).

"Attraction of the World" (*Atração do Mundo*), to use the famous phrase by Joaquim Nabuco. Silviano Santiago later deconstructs Nabuco's optimism by making evident his marginal testimony of world events and simultaneously denouncing his disregard for the political and cultural reality of the country.

The bipolarity between the two perspectives, one looking at the inclusion of Brazil in the world and the other committed to the reality of the country, prefigures the contemporary condition of the Brazilian authors and artists who are recognized in this margin, in this periphery of a world submitted to a hegemonic Western globalization. To assume the impossibility of a dialectical synthesis between hegemonic globalization and the peripheral nation means to assume the margin, a point of departure for another global projection—for Santiago via a "cosmopolitanism of the poor"—which is not hegemonic and maintains the irreconcilable difference between the extremes, but whose dichotomous structure can be inverted through strategic political wagers. Without seeking synthesis, the contemporary author finds himself or herself caught between an increasing global coexistence—a result of a certain international circulation through editions in translation and participation in fairs around the world—and the circumstances of everyday interaction with the national market, the national media and readers often trapped in their mother tongue. The attempts to overcome the boundary between these two perspectives in most cases are doomed to failure, there being few writers who achieve international distribution today,[9] and whoever does, as in the case of Paulo Coelho, does so at the cost of his or her national recognition. Contemporary literature exists, in this sense, between two opposite forces, between what Mariano Siskind, in the book *Cosmopolitan Desires: Global Modernity and World Literature in Latin America* (2014), with insightful sensibility called the "globalization of the novel," on the one hand, and, on the other, the "novelization of the global."

---

[9] According to Luciana Villas-Boas, in an interview given to the *Folha de São Paulo* newspaper on February 23, 2014, "Brazilian authors are obsessed with translation. The translation of their own works, actually. There are no awards, readerly praise or even good sales in Brazil that compare to the validation of their texts by a foreign publisher. If possible, their translation into English, but exotic versions also serve, such as into Serbian or Romanian, editions with no monetary significance and that reach around 300 readers. They give the impression that one is going far." ("O autor brasileiro é vidrado numa tradução. Tradução de sua própria obra, bem entendido. Não há prêmio, elogio de leitor nem sequer boas vendas no Brasil que se comparem à validação de seu texto por uma editora estrangeira. Se possível, a tradução para o inglês, mas servem versões exóticas, como para o sérvio ou o romeno, edições sem significado monetário e que atingem uns 300 leitores. Dão a impressão que se está chegando longe.") https://www1.folha.uol.com.br/ilustrissima/2014/02/1415721-para-quem-escreve-o-autor-local.shtml.

During the past few decades of economic stability until the onset of the economic crises in 2014, the publishing industry in expansion[10] underwent a process of international recognition that resulted in the absorption of several Brazilian publishers by large multinational publishing corporations, which for writers opened new doors for the diffusion of their books in other languages.[11] This economic process had been accompanied by public incentives for the publication of national literature, for example, through the translation support given by the Brazilian National Library and through the investment in international book fairs, which gave Brazilian authors the furtive taste of international breakthrough. These processes indicated one more step in the globalization of the novel, which expanded during the eighteenth and nineteenth centuries along with colonization, and whose market parameters still prevail in Brazil, where American authors easily surpass Brazilian ones on best-seller lists.

The other side of the coin is more interesting to analyze in the present context. To "novelize the global" means using literature, fiction and the novel to create images of the global world. Thus, just as Benedict Anderson spoke of the importance of an "imagined community," which was constitutive for the nation, in the process of modernization, one should consider a global imaginary supported by a cartography of the world and by the cosmopolitan projection that operate in Brazilian novels today. How do writers recognize themselves from the perspective of a fictional world in transit between the nation and the world, and between the margin and the center? If one inverts, for the sake of argument, Machado de Assis's analysis of the Brazilian writer, one may understand the cosmopolitan writer as an artist who expresses his or her estrangement in the face of what is most familiar in terms of national experience, even when he or she exercises estranged intimacy in the globalized world at hand. Thus, the artist or writer becomes contemporary as a result of a difference, a critical rejection, which allows him or her to capture his or her time and see it as biased or as an intersection. It does not therefore concern representing the present, unless by an inadequacy, a historical estrangement that reveals the marginal and obscure zones of the present that distance themselves from the predominant tendency. To be contemporary is to be capable

---

[10] Between 1990 and 2014 the number of titles increased from 22,479 to 60,829 and the sales from 212 million to 435 million.

[11] In 2005 the Spanish publisher Grupo Santilliana, owner of Editora Moderna, bought 76 percent of the Objetiva publishing house, and in 2011 Penguin assumed 45 percent of the shares of Companhia das Letras. Then, Random House absorbed Penguin and parts of Santilliana and Companhia das Letras thus became the new owner of Objetiva. In April 2020, Random House were absorbed by the German Bertelsmann.

of finding one's way without identification, and thus of having the courage to recognize and commit to a present with which it is not possible to coincide.

There are two facets of this imaginary relation to the world. In the 1990s, João Gilberto Noll introduces, in the novels *Harmada* (1993) and *Céu Aberto* (Open sky, 1996), a narrative in which national characteristics dissolve in an uncertain geography without defined landscapes. In the later novels, *Berkeley em Bellagio* (Berkeley in Bellagio, 2002) and *Lorde* (2004), Noll restages the travel narrative by fictionalizing two autobiographical trips, his seminar in Bellagio, Italy, and his writing residency at King's College in London. In the face of the foreign, the classic figure of the conquering traveler in these novels is inverted into a feeling of lack of belonging and sharp loss of personal and cultural identity aggravated by the cosmopolitan challenge. What seems to be the confirmation of an unprecedented access to world scenarios is converted into a testimony of the dissolution of both national and cosmopolitan identitarian cultural characteristics. In the same way, in the first novel by Alexandre Vidal Porto, *Sergio Y.*, the trip to New York by the young Sergio Y. is, in theory, the way to change his life, a possibility of being happy, by leaving the protection of his family, the comfort of a rich kid in São Paulo, and mainly his sexual identity. Protected by the anonymity of the cosmopolitan city, Sergio becomes Sandra and begins what would be a new and fulfilling life, were it not for the fatal fall from a window that ends the story prematurely and enigmatically.

The turn of the twenty-first century brought to the fictional scene a traveler with a great potential for movement and for whom international trips led to interrogations on self-identity, which can be observed more clearly in the novels of Bernardo Carvalho—*Mongólia* (2003) and *Filho da Mãe* (Son of a mother, 2009). But, in the end, the search is frustrated, as in the novel *O Céu se põe em São Paulo* (The sun sets in São Paulo, 2007), a "story of outcasts, such as myself and mine own, people who can't belong to the place where they are, wherever they are, and dream of another place, that can only exist in the imagination."[12] Bernardo Carvalho here exposes what Mariano Siskind has called a critical cosmopolitanism in his articulation of the impossibility of assuming an identity fixed in a particular place, whether national or not. Some of these novels from the first decade of the new century expressed the general national optimism and the confidence of an aggressive Brazilian tourism that, driven by a strong national currency, a strong national border, and a search for an international role in the global political scene, expressed a

---

[12] The original in Portuguese reads: "história de párias, como eu e os meus, gente que não pode pertencer ao lugar onde está, onde quer que esteja, e sonha com outro lugar, que só pode existir na imaginação."

new cosmopolitan desire whose facility paradoxically exposed the identitarian weakness of national characteristics.

For the sake of argument, there are also other novels in which the foreign experience makes the other side of globalization emerge, a marginal point of view that illuminates contemporary Brazilian society through the gaze of a reflexive anthropology that recognizes the otherness of its own culture. There arises in novels such as *O paraíso é bem bacana* (Paradise is really cool, 2006) and in short stories such as "O Brasil é Bom" (Brazil is good, 2014), by André Sant'anna, a prose in which the characters articulate the most grotesque aspects of their own reality through the prism of estrangement, alienation and lack of identification on the part of the traveler. The account of the football player from Ubatuba who signs a professional contract with the German club Herta Berlin, where he becomes the suicide bomber Mané Muhammed, is a sort of sinister caricature of the promises of globalization. It also simultaneously exposes the futility of the dreams of the Western world and the emptying of Brazilian culture in its most everyday cultural and linguistic substance.

In a recent survey in the *Ilustríssimo* section of the *Folha de São Paulo* newspaper, several critics responded to the question of whether national identity, a theme that was always present in fiction, had been lost and was no longer central. The São Paulo critic Alcir Pécora responded that the question "of identity was only one of the possibilities of thinking about experienced events with relative urgency."[13] More important was that,

> Until around the 1960s-1970s, literary form was central for Brazilian critics. It seemed central in the consistent creation of an imaginary community that answered for Brazil or for its purposes. Today, this interpretative urgency has given way to the representation of a small spectacle of itself, of groups of readers, or of more restricted communities, with tastes and perspectives that are homogenous a priori, despite being disseminated throughout the world. I mean to say, anyway, that it does not seem to be in literature, in the language of invention, that one wages, today, the battle of reality's contradictions or of the search for its more consistent alternatives.[14]

---

[13] The original in Portuguese reads: "da identidade era apenas uma das possibilidades de pensar os acontecimentos vividos com relativa urgência."

[14] The original in Portuguese reads: "A questão, até por volta dos anos 60/70, era outra: a forma literária era central na interpretação do país. A forma literária parecia a todos os escritores uma questão central em favor da criação de uma comunidade imaginária que respondia pelo Brasil ou pelo seu destino como país. Hoje, essa urgência interpretativa

This critical interrogation by Pécora merits attention as a warning, for contemporary literature, of the threat of losing the centrality and privilege of being the focus of interrogation in the reality in which it is included. Despite partially agreeing, I shall introduce a few examples of possible exceptions to this diagnosis, which indicate the effects of the growing commercial globalization of literature in response to the ever more vivid experience of the international transitions and shifts that affect everyday life, particularly that of the Brazilian middle-class, the main producer of national literature.

In 2003, the Teatro da Vertigem (Vertigo Theater) group prepared perhaps its most ambitious project: *BR3: Brasilândia—Brasília—Brasiléia*. After its biblical trilogy (*Apocalipse 1:11*), the Teatro da Vertigem's project delves further into the question of Brazilian identity and national character. Always working in a theoretical and practical way, the group, on the one hand, studied the country's great intellectuals, such as Gilberto Freyre, Sérgio Buarque de Hollanda, Caio Prado Júnior, Raymundo Faoro, Darcy Ribeiro and Milton Santos. On the other hand, it made a geographical journey through three different "Brasis": Brasilândia (a neighborhood on the periphery of the city of São Paulo), Brasília (the nation's capital, situated in the center of the country) and Brasiléia (a city at the far end of Acre, almost on the border with Bolivia). Thus, it attempted to reformulate the national question from a contemporary perspective of the periphery in three dimensions: of the city (in the Brasilândia of São Paulo), of the nation (in the Brasiléia of Acre) and of Brazilian society (in Brasília, the national center, which is also an international periphery). As the group explains:

> If, 500 years later, we can no longer *dis*cover Brazil, we can at least *un*cover (or rather expose) a certain Brazil. And beyond a mapping or recognition of a character, identity, or country, we hope that such a journey serves also as a guide, a beacon, a compass for the creation—and re-creation—of identities and territories.[15]

---

perdeu fôlego para a representação de um pequeno espetáculo de si, de grupos de leitores ou de comunidades mais restritas, com gostos e perspectivas homogêneos, ainda que disseminados pela internet—, que, hoje, também sabemos que está longe de cumprir os sonhos de descentralização e de democracia que lhe atribuíram os seus apologistas. Enfim, quero dizer: não me parece que seja na literatura, na linguagem da invenção, que se trava, hoje, a batalha das contradições do real ou da busca de suas alternativas mais consistentes."

[15] The original in Portuguese reads: "Se, 500 anos depois, já não podemos mais descobrir o Brasil, que ao menos possamos des-cobrir *(ou seja expor)* um certo Brasil. E que mais do que um mapeamento ou reconhecimento de um caráter, identidade ou país, esperamos que tal jornada nos sirva também como norte, como farol, como bússola para a criação—e re-criação—de identidades e territórios."

After several months of work with the local community of Brasilândia, the group prepared the performance on a bus trip to Brasiléia, a route that lasted one month and ended with the staging of the play on ferryboats on the Tietê River in São Paulo, and later in the Guanabara Bay of Rio de Janeiro.

The globalized or internationalized condition of the Brazilian writer is expressed in a certain inversion of typically national scenarios. In the recent novel by Marcelino Freire, *Nossos Ossos* (Our bones, 2013), the narrator is a Northeasterner and playwright who lives in São Paulo and whose lover, a male prostitute who is also from the Northeast, is murdered in an obscure and poorly explained situation. After this event, which evokes death as a primordial cause of the story, the narrative proceeds in two directions: an almost detective-like movement that reconstructs the final hours of the victim, and a retrospective of the love story between the two that, in the materiality of the text, conjugates the temporalities of memory with the present of action and the project of future redemption for the body. In a sort of road movie, the narrator proposes to take the corpse back to its family in the Northeast and begins a trip to his geographical and cultural origins. Only, this physical return route is not gratuitous and the trip ends up unleashing an existential deepening of the identity crises of the narrator, who is fatally led to suicide. There is thus an attempted repetition of the stories of Northeastern migration to the big cities that, in the 1950s and 1960s, was the big motive in a Brazilian regionalist literature that evoked the urban destiny of the industrially developing country. Now, however, such a destiny is inverted, which thereby calls for a necessary contemporary reflection on the regional and cultural issues of Brazil. Today, one asserts the recognition of the centrality of the peripheral condition as one of the main features of current globalization. More than able to homogenize Western cultural conditions by extending the privileges of economic and cultural centers, contemporaneity is characterized by the proliferation of the peripheral condition that already emerges in the misery encountered everywhere, despite efforts to the contrary. Cultural, racial and social otherness is no longer on the horizon of the foreign, but is reintroduced at the heart of everyday Western life, as the experience of exteriority threatens the hierarchy of civilizing values.

The inventor of German systems theory, Niklas Luhmann (1992), identified modernity with the epistemological condition of "second-level observer," who, unlike the "first-level observer," possesses the privilege of Cartesian self-reflexivity. The observing subject, in the face of his or her object, reflects on his or her own position of observer and "sees" himself or herself "seeing." Today, in the global condition reflected by contemporary literature, the observing subject loses his or her centrality, since it is the observed that begins to observe, being already seen and objectified by another gaze that has lost its center and is everywhere. One can perhaps understand these examples not as realist representations of the social and cultural conditions of the country, but as a realism that expresses an unperceived and latent dimension that is not directly proven in the everyday or in historical or anthropological studies, as Luiz Costa Lima suggests in a text about the novel of the new millennium. "Nineteenth century realism," Luiz Costa Lima (2011) writes in "No Novo Milênio: Um novo romance?" (In the new millenium, a new novel?), "was founded in the evident, but what is now shown highlights the latent. What may be a new tendency in the novel is not opposed to the dominance of the fictional. Everything takes place as if between reality and fiction there had been only a wall, and that it has collapsed."[16] This latency is constituted by globalized scenarios that assume the periphery and offer resistance to the single dialectics (the *one* and the *unequal*, of which Moretti speaks), as well as materialize the globalized condition in an ethical landscape in which encounters take place and initiate a challenge of political resistance that refers to the fight against inequality, actualizing its real possibility of inversion not as a reversal of inevitable globalization, but as its micropolitical and local response.

To conclude, the argument has been for a contemporary perspectivism that values the margin as a platform for a sharp criticism, not only of Brazilian national wounds in the postcolonial world, but also of the hegemonic operation of the globalized world, whose globalizing project is revealed to be strongly selective and unequal. A synthetic reconciliation of these two dimensions seems to be a distant and, in most cases, undesirable possibility. One should perhaps recognize that the difference between the dialectical perspective of a desired synthesis of the modernization project and the exclusionary Brazilian social reality, and a marginality that is assumed and irreconcilable before the unjust global scenario, possesses a critical potential that was characterized by the Japanese philosopher Kojin Karatani as a "parallax view." When faced with an antimony in the Kantian sense, Karatani writes, one should renounce any dialectical synthesis of opposites. Slavoj Žižek (2004) revives and expands this philosophical argument to situate the contemporary possibility of radical critique, not in the taking of one certain position in detriment to the other, but in the assertion of the irreducible difference between them. One should not see things either from one point of view or the other, but face the reality exposed through this difference, the parallax, by accepting the antinomic character of the experience of reality.

---

[16] The original in Portuguese reads: "O realismo do século 19 [...] fundava-se no patente, o que agora se mostra destaca o latente. O que suponho ser uma nova tendência do romance não se opõe à dominância do ficcional. Tudo se passa como se entre o real e o ficcional tivesse havido tão só uma parede; e que ela desabou."

If antimony, in Kant, marked the insurmountable difference between the phenomenon and the thing in itself (*Ding an Sich*), the paradox for us occurs between the universal of humanism and the particular of national experience. Likewise, the thing in itself, the universal, is not something transcendental beyond perception, but that which, according to Spivak, one may characterize as a planetary dimension only discernible as a result of the antimonic character of the experience of reality. One needs, as Žižek has said, to maintain the separation of the two levels, and one cannot use the same language to characterize phenomena that are mutually untranslatable and that can only be perceived through a parallax view, which constantly changes perspective between the two without synthesis or mediation. Nonetheless, Žižek points out that the thing in itself, after Lacan, can only be thought in its traumatic dimension, which today is revealed as the irreconcilable abyss between the declaration of human rights and the reality of walls and barbed wire that close the borders in the face of the waves of African and Arab refugees. To preserve this double perspective means to commit oneself to what Aby Warburg has called an "iconology of intervals," this space in between (*Zwischenraum*) constituted by the relations between differences in permanent conflict, between the *monstra* and the *astra* or between culture and barbarianism.

Chapter 7

THE CHALLENGE OF THE SENSIBLE AND THE SUBLIME REVISITED

In the presentation of the book *The Anti-Aesthetic: Essays on Postmodern Culture*, the editor Hal Foster (1983) explains the use of the concept of "anti-aesthetic" for the collection of essays that, in 1984, opened the discussion on the postmodern, with contributions that encompassed differences that ranged from Jürgen Habermas to Jean Baudrillard, passing through Rosalind Krauss, Fredric Jameson and Edward Saïd, among others. All of these critics, Foster says, agree on the observation that we are never outside of "representation," or rather, we never avoid its politics. Thus, the "anti-aesthetic" does not indicate the modern and transgressive nihilism whose rupture with the law and language only serves to affirm them. On the contrary, the anti-aesthetic should be understood as a "critique which destructures the order of representations in order to reinscribe them" (Foster 1983, xv). At the same time, the title evidently questions the notion of *aesthetic*, or the idea that the aesthetic experience exists in autonomy, without purpose, or outside of history. It is the demand for an art capable of affecting the world, an art which is simultaneously "(inter)subjective, concrete and universal—a symbolic totality" (Foster 1983). Besides the questioning of traditional aesthetic categories, the anti-aesthetic signals, from the perspective of the postmodern, a transdisciplinary practice that interacts with politically committed cultural forms by rejecting the idea of a privileged aesthetic sphere. For Foster, the aesthetic should be considered another of the *grand narratives* of modernity, beginning with idealist autonomy and ending with its status of a necessarily critical category. Such a critique is directed at the instrumental world, as in the work of Adorno, in which the aesthetic has the critical potency of a negative and subversive intervention in the face of capitalism and its alienated consumer culture.

When Foster's collection was published, the more politicized postmodern was interpreted as an antidote against the similar modern confidence in the negative power of art. The implicit demand was for it to be substituted by notions of interference and resistance, within a critical recognition of the limitations of the actual domain of the aesthetic. One must first observe that the anti-aesthetic, therefore, seemed to accompany the aesthetic in a peculiar and significant way. As indicated by James Elkins (2013), the aesthetic has been understood almost as a synonym of modernism, but at the same time, the anti-aesthetic already described modernism's reaction against academic art at the turn of the twentieth century. In this sense, it would come to accompany and characterize the critical practice of vanguard modernism. It is this critical sense that was preserved by the anti-aesthetic in the past century, through its accentuation of a possible anticapitalist radicalness in more politicized art. Even so, the aesthetic continues to exist in contemporary art, in which it describes and identifies an appreciation of more traditional practices in the artistic disciplines—painting, sculpture, photography and so on—that still preserve the creation of works and the attribution of value to professional artistic practice as it interacts with museums, galleries and the market. In sum, one may understand the anti-aesthetic not only as a tool of a politically committed art, but also as that which uses the rupture of aesthetic beauty to aim at other effects, such as astonishment, rejection, ugliness, distaste, disgust and shock. That is why there is no radical contradiction between the aesthetic and the anti-aesthetic; most contemporary artists make use of both, such as the many who consider themselves committed both to art and to politics.

Mario Perniola (2013) observes, in a book from the end of the past century, that it is not common to consider the twentieth century the century of aesthetics.

> Nevertheless, in the first half of the twentieth century, aesthetics has claimed to be more than just the philosophical theory of the beautiful and good taste. On the one hand, it has established a relation of complicity with literature, the figurative arts and music without letting itself be scared by the most daring innovations and the riskiest experimentations; on the other hand, it had been involved in the management of institutions, exhibitions, the organization and the communication of artistic and cultural products. It has confronted the great problems of the single and collective life, it has questioned itself on the sense of existence, it has promoted daring social utopias, it has been involved in the issues of everyday life and has singled out subtle cognitive distinctions. (Perniola 2013, 1)

Perniola organizes this variety of manifestations of an aesthetic thinking into four domains, or conceptual fields, identified by the notions of "life, form, knowledge, and action." These are the concepts that come to organize the discussion presented in the book, even though, since the beginning, they point to an end to these fields in the second half of the twentieth century with the following tendency: "(1) the aesthetic of life acquires a political significance; (2) the aesthetics of form a media one; the aesthetic of knowledge a skeptical one; and (3) pragmatic aesthetics a communicative one." In other words, Perniola distinguishes a philosophy of *life*, as in the post-structuralist philosophy of, for example, Giorgio Agamben, one of *form*, as in Marshall McLuhan or in the sublime of Jean-François Lyotard, an aesthetic of *knowledge*, as in, for example, Nelson Goodman or Gianni Vattimo, and a *pragmatic* aesthetics, as in the communicative action of Jürgen Habermas and in the ironic action of Richard Rorty. For Perniola, these four tendencies were all maintained within the fundamental premises of Kant and Hegel, mainly because they all pointed to a dialectical reconciliation of opposites, the sensible and the intelligible, and to the intellectual appropriation of aesthetic experience.

In the twentieth century, there nonetheless appears an element of which aesthetics is not capable of taking into account and which is paradoxically presented as that which should be the actual center of aesthetic reflection: feeling. In feeling, the Italian philosopher identifies a contradiction that is greater than the dialectical contradiction and that must be seen in light of the notion of difference, understood as nonidentity, a radical dissemblance that points outside of Hegelian dialectics and Aristotelian identity. It is, Perniola says, "the impure one [sphere] of feeling, of uncommon and uncanny experiences, irreducible to identity, ambivalent and excessive, of which the existence of many men and women of the twentieth century has been intertwined" (110). Feeling is, in other words, too different from that sensible which constituted the point of departure for the aesthetics of Kant and Hegel. Only with the thinking of Freud did the reflection on the sensible seem to move in a particularly anti-aesthetic direction, for, by situating the conflicts between the human and nature inside the actual human being, the father of psychoanalysis introduces "separation and chaos, malaise and ugliness, suffering and abjection into an affectivity that in Kant swayed between the sentiment of the beautiful and the sublime, and in Hegel between the *pathos* of the spirit and the creation of the artistic ideal" (112). Perniola thus introduces an understanding of the anti-aesthetic as a result of the problem of *difference*, from which one further explores unknown zones of feeling that are no longer reduced to the conceptual devices of nineteenth-century philosophy and aesthetics. In the twentieth century, Perniola observes, literature and art begin to seek inspiration in a radical sensibility of experiences that are deviant, mystical, ecstatic, perverse, primitive and alternative in other ways.

It is the Freudian analysis of the unconscious that discovers an otherness that is not domesticated by reason, as can be observed in the essays on wit (*Witz*) and on the uncanny (*Unheimliche*). From Perniola's perspective, psychoanalysis thus clears the way for a series of philosophers, from Heidegger to

Bataille, passing through Wittgenstein, Benjamin, Shklovsky, Blanchot and Klossowski, and culminating in Lacan, Irigaray, Deleuze and Derrida, among others, who are all guided by the challenge of considering a radical feeling that contests any conceptualization or form attributed by thought. Freud discovers the "greatest difference, the farthest experience from identity. Not absolute extraneousness but a familiar one which has its roots in our past, which is and is not itself at the same time" (Perniola 2013, 115). In Kant's aesthetics, the notion of the sublime is of particular interest for its dynamic tension with the beautiful. But it concerns, in Kant's theoretical architecture, an idealized experience in which the negative potential is totally sublimated, just as the representation of evil can be assimilated and purified by art. To follow the recognition of the negative pleasures in Kant, only the concept of *disgust* escapes this assimilation. Thus, Kant individualizes the opposite of taste in disgust, *distaste*, which seems to be the unnamable, the unrepresentable and the absolutely different.

In this sense, it is not by chance that Hal Foster, some years after the success mentioned earlier, publishes a book whose impact was particularly great, precisely for considering the anti-aesthetic from the perspective of trauma and its shock effect, which will somehow appropriate the centrality of aesthetic pleasure in the Kantian analysis of the beautiful. Where Kant situated the driving cause of judgment of the beautiful, in disinterested pleasure before the work, Foster points to a fissure, a wound, which affectively causes a traumatic effect. Today one perceives how Hal Foster, at that time, opened a way out of the antimonies of the postmodern moment and prepared a field for the historical view of the contemporary, with a broad acceptance of the complex anachronistic relations that characterize the present. For example, there is the discussion of the concept of repetition that Foster pursues to consider the idea of a return of the historical avant-garde in the postwar neo-avant-garde. By criticizing Peter Bürger's classic study, *Theory of the Avant-Garde* (1984), in which the neo-avant-garde is considered a pathetic and opportunistic parallel of the historical avant-garde, Foster embellishes his argument with the famous quote by Marx: "all great events of world history occur twice, the first time as tragedy, the second time as farce" (Foster 1996, 14). The alternative presented by Foster is a paradoxical image of time which allows one to recognize that, when the "avant-garde recedes into the past, it also returns from the future, repositioned by innovative art in the present" (Foster 1996, X). This strange notion of temporality is a free appropriation of the interpretations that Jacques Lacan and Laplanche make of the temporal model used by Freud in his explanation of trauma. The psychic system is not prepared to absorb the trauma, whose repeated symptom serves as preparation for posterior recognition.

With this parallel, Foster suggests a historical model in which historical events will only be recognized a posteriori in a *deferred action* (*Nachträglichkeit*) that somehow recodifies what at first was only recorded in gross fashion:

> Historical and neo-avant-gardes are constituted in a similar way, as a continual process of protension and retension, a complex relay of anticipated futures and reconstructed pasts-in short, in a deferred action that throws over any simple scheme of before and after, cause and effect, origin and repetition. (Foster 1996, 29)

To simplify, Foster's idea is that works of New York Dada in 1917 (Duchamp's urinal) and of Russian Constructivism in 1921 (Rodchenko's monochromes), to give only a few of the examples analyzed, somehow only gained their critical and institutional dimension as a consequence of works 50 years later by the Belgian conceptual artist Marcel Broodthaers and by the American minimalist Daniel Buren. A large part of the book's importance is a result of this wish to propose alternatives to the fossilized interpretations of the movements of the 1960s and 1970s. The study of the impact on art, at the height of semiological theories, gains general relevance by showing how the emergence, in art, of an interest in indexical marks and allegorical impulses is nourished by post-structural questioning. With the idea of a "return of the real," Foster seeks to avoid what he perceives as the two predominant representational models in the criticism of the final decades of the twentieth century: the *referential* model, on the one hand, and the *simulacral* model, on the other, which both unfold in the traditional antagonism between "realist" art and pop art. The first model, Foster says, understands images and signs as connected to referents, to iconographic themes or things that are real in the world of experience. In the second, all images are considered mere representations of other images, a view that converts the whole representational system, including realism, into a self-referential system. But why not think of contemporary representation as *referential* and *simulacral* at the same time, as a creation of images that are not only connected to reality, but also disconnected, that are simultaneously real and artificial, affective and cold, critical and complacent?

For Hal Foster, it is this challenge of understanding the coexistence of the two modes of representation that appears in the work of Andy Warhol, which is clearly visible in the *Death and Disaster* series. Through its repetitive use of shocking images from the press, for example, of traffic accidents or lynchings, Warhol's series produces the impact that Foster calls a *traumatic realism*. Here, realism is no longer the effect of representation, but a "trauma event," an image of social and political violence affectively marked by the limit of what can or cannot be represented. It is an image that becomes an index and archive of this same impossibility, and it insinuates a greater referentiality that explains the centrality of the archive and of anthropology in artistic movements of the 1980s and 1990s. It is important to emphasize that Foster's perspective, though initially connected to an extreme phenomenon found in the plastic arts, has quickly gained force in the interpretation of a contemporary passion for the real that is much more comprehensive and that covers all the arts from literature to cinema and the visual and performing arts in general, emphasizing documentary, testimonial, performative, relational and indexical aspects in direct and often polemical and promiscuous competition with the massive demand for reality in media culture.

In his already mentioned book *Malaise dans l'esthetique* (2004a), the philosopher Jacques Rancière sought to diagnose the symptoms of contemporary aesthetics through a dialogue with the aforementioned questions and by proposing two central views of the post-utopian present of art. In the first place, Rancière describes a current tendency among philosophers and art historians to separate the artistic search from the utopian dreams of a new life, as a result of the failure of these utopias in authoritarian projects or in aesthetic commercialization. Instead of this failed alliance, the radicalness of art is accentuated in its singular power to create effects of presence in its appearance and inscription. From this point of view, Rancière recognizes the survival of the Kantian sublime in the heterogeneous and irreducible presence of a force of the sensible that destroys and exceeds the imagination and understanding. This point will be discussed here later. In the second place, one observes among artists and art professionals another tendency that distances itself simultaneously from aesthetic utopias and from the artistic radicalness exalted in the first tendency. Here there are no illusions about the transformative power of art or about the singularity of the work. This tendency's perspective is that of relational art or conceptual art, which with all modesty rearranges the objects that compose the world in its everyday and common reality. It is an art that performs small alterations with the purpose of modifying perception and possibilities of action with respect to this collective environment. In both perspectives, one encounters clearly anti-aesthetic performances. If, on the one hand, it concerns an art of the sublime in which the power of art reveals its potency through the distance that it establishes in relation to common experience, on the other, it concerns a relational art in which there are modest forms of a micropolitics in the density of the everyday that subtly reorganize the common world. Examining the perspective of the sublime, Rancière recognizes the exaltation of the power of the work to establish a being in common and prior to the various forms of politics, such as the *Look!* Exhibit from 2001, which was curated by Thierry de Duve and which revived the belief in Christian communion through the incarnation of the word. Nonetheless, he also identifies the Jewish prohibition of representations of God, in which the sublime marks an abyss between the idea and the sensible.

That is how Rancière sees the philosopher Jean-François Lyotard represent his understanding of the role of modern art in the testimony of the unrepresentable and in the search for a singularity of appearance that thus converts the artistic gesture into a negative presentation. Lyotard identifies the art of the avant-garde with the Kantian sublime, for the avant-garde is able to manifest the sublime to the extent that it is directed against the beautiful appearance of forms and proposes to affirm the presence of that which avoids representation, that is, to testify to the unrepresentable. But Lyotard remains in immanence and does not follow the spiritualist interpretation of form in the transcendence of the idea. The sublime is able to mediate an experience of the absolute through the insufficiency of form in the subtle materiality of its infinite variations. Thus, Lyotard attributes to the art of the avant-garde "the paradoxical task of manifesting the immateriality of the sublime through matter. This materiality can only be 'minimal'" (Perniola 2013, 55).

Already in 1988, in the text "Après le sublime, était de l'ésthetique," which was written at the height of the debates on the postmodern, Lyotard describes the post-Romantic experience of the sublime, in which it is no longer the unrepresentable in the idea that emerges with the defeat of the imagination, as Kant's analysis indicated, but the *deferring* of *nuance* and *timbre* at the heart of sensible materiality that destabilizes the classificatory concept of the note or tone. It is in this minimal space of a note or a color that

> timbre and nuance introduce a sort of infinity, the indeterminacy of the harmonics within the frame determined by this identity. Nuance or timbre are the distress and despair of the exact division and thus the clear composition of sounds and colors according to graded scales and harmonic temperaments. (Lyotard 1991a, 140)

Thus, Lyotard distances himself from the idealist and dialectical interpretation of the sublime and situates concentrated aesthetic experience in the sensible, in the affirmation of the presence of something unnamable—the nuances of a sound or color—that cannot be manifested except through sensations.

On this point, one may observe that the aesthetic power of art, for Lyotard, stems from the sensible and abandons the transcendence that Kant identified in the sublime and that ended up confirming the superiority of the idea of reason. For Kant, the sublime translates the imagination's incapacity to conceive a monument in its totality, and it does not refer to a work of art. Like human impotence when threatened by the savage forces of nature, the imagination for Kant is defeated in the face of the task of presenting totality to reason, and this defeat leads us from aesthetics to the moral domain, for it becomes a negative sign of the supremacy of reason over nature and of its legislative vocation in the supersensible order. In Lyotard's reading, the sublime is not only a result of force or size; its power is in the sensible itself, as a presence without appeal in terms of presentation. It concerns, then, matter in its otherness, but how can this otherness be conceived? Materiality is pure difference, according to Lyotard, a difference not determined by conceptualizations such as timbre and nuance, whose singularity is in contrast with the infinite game of differences and determinations that govern musical compositions or the harmony of colors. Lyotard refers to this irreducible difference as "immateriality," or an "immaterial materiality."

Besides singularity, the second characteristic of this immateriality is its power to make suffer (*faire patir*), to become an event of passion for all. Two observations are appropriate here. Immateriality is characterized, for Lyotard, by the unavailability of the conceptual form, a feature that for Kant was part of his analysis of the beautiful. The judgment of beauty refers to a form that is not conceptual form imposing its unity on the diversity of sensations. Beauty is beautiful because it is neither an object of knowledge nor an object of desire. It is this unavailability of a form—*das Unform, die Formlosigkeit*—for the faculties of understanding and desire that allows the subject to experience a new autonomy. What supports "aesthetic feeling is no longer the free synthesis of forms by the imagination," Lyotard writes, "but the failure to synthesize" (Lyotard 1988, 41). Form is no longer the crucial issue of aesthetic feeling, which eliminates the importance of the faculty of the imagination and refers directly to the idea of reason. On the other hand, immateriality is characterized by the disruptive power of the formless, a specific feature of rupture that for Kant belonged to the sublime and that is presented as a negative sign of the idea of reason.

> With the aesthetics of the sublime it can be argued that a kind of progress in human history is possible which would not be only the progress of technology and science available to mankind. It is indeed not a progress of the beautiful, of the taste in beauty, but of the responsibility to the Ideas of reason as they are negatively "presented" in the formlessness of such and such a situation which could occur. (Lyotard 1988, 41)

In a certain way, Lyotard brings the power of the sublime back to the domain of art, and it would be the avant-garde that would assume the task of giving presence to the unrepresentable by radically referring not only to alienation but also to the inaugural shock of a disaster whose wound is irreconcilably in the difference and sensible otherness of materiality. In the context of the 1980s, at the height of the postmodern eclecticism in which different languages mixed—the abstract with the figurative in painting, the conceptual with the lyrical in writing—, the limits between commercial images and artistic ones were confused and the power of language rupture was dismantled, which had been the common focus of representational subversion by the historical avant-garde. One should recognize Lyotard's efforts to identify a potential for rupture in a material and sensible otherness, an energy that was also sought in the intensities and enthusiasm of language games or in the emergence of immaterial networks supported by new technologies,[1] and that, through the presentation of the unnamable, referred to a condition of shock and disaster in modernity itself.

For Lyotard, to give testimony to the unrepresentable—*le différend*—was to situate in the sensible an immanent power of difference. In the contemporary, a figure gained broad acceptance via the notion of affect. Affects are intensities provoked in the body and by the body, or, as Spinoza says, are the effect that another body or object, a work of art for instance, has on my body and its duration. The affect operates on the pre-individual level without necessarily being on the pre-social level, and the affective circumstance is a sensible element in experience that anticipates the subject and its meaning. From this perspective, it is more fundamental than emotion, which already contains an interpretation. For theorists such as Gilles Deleuze and Félix Guattari, affects operate on the *molecular* level prior and subjacent to the molar foundations of representation. In this sense, one articulates an understanding of art as frozen affects and perceptions, *blocks of sensations*, which will be activated with intensity by the interaction with the spectator. One may ask why the theory of affects has gained enormous attention in the contemporary, and answer that this probably has to do with the cultural condition of media culture, which imposes immediately present sensations of images and representations in real time and offers interaction with complex networks of connectivity that involve bodies in a preconscious and affective manner. We somehow live in a dimension of public intimacy in which the social event becomes real to the extent that it is subjectively internalized and the subject is affirmed inasmuch as it is mirrored in public recognition.

Brian Massumi's research takes the media as an object of analysis, and since the 1990s, essays such as "The Autonomy of Affect" (1995) have led a substantial part of research on the contemporary conditions of media culture.

---

[1] See, for example, the exhibition at the Centre Pompidou, *Les Immatériaux* (1985), curated by Jean-François Lyotard.

In Massumi's seminal essay, affect is described as the domain of intensity, indetermination and potentiality qualified by cultural logic. It is in cultural mediation, in encounters, that affect circulates and is incorporated even prior to the subjective constitution of the person. That is why affect is different than emotion, for the latter is conscious and symbolized by the subject, while affect conditions the body in the social process of subjectification. Much prior to appearing in subjective consciousness as emotion, affect is inscribed in bodies in traces of past encounters and actions that lead the body via intensities to the actualization of certain potentialities. Thus, the body is always a social body, which circulates among affective intensities, on the one hand, and discursive mediations, on the other. For Lyotard, art has the power to cause one to suffer from attraction to it, to make one fall in love with it, as a result of its sensible excess, its rapture and impersonal power, which are converted into an event capable of interacting with the senses in a way that can not only corroborate with its reception but also deviate from it productively. Affects are these moments of intensity that produce reactions in the body and through the body at a level that is immanent to the sensible, immanent to experience and prior to the semiotic constitution of meaning.

Chapter 8
FAREWELL TO THE CONTEMPORARY!

Upon finishing this book on contemporary fiction in Brazil, it is difficult to avoid a feeling of farewell! In 2020, the political, economic and social situation in Brazil has become so aggravated that it has eclipsed a certain optimistic view that guided most of my readings of the literary production of the past few years. In the face of the neopopulist turn that brought President Jair Bolsonaro to power at the beginning of 2019, the public sphere has become tense and an aggressive polarization of opinions has perpetrated the hardened climate of constant election fighting and diminished the possibility of a serious discussion about the social, environmental and cultural challenges that threaten the country.

For the past five years, Brazil has been undergoing an aggravated economic and institutional crisis of harsh cuts in education and culture that threaten to halt or restrict research in the country and dismantle the cultural support system in the name of economic necessity, on the one hand, and the desire for ideological repression, on the other. Brazilians have been submitted to the control of a right-wing government that sees itself imbued with the mission to eliminate what has been built in the country since the democratization in 1985 in terms of the fight against inequality and the right of expression of cultural and political diversity. During the past few years, the population has begun to live under the threat of a series of disasters as a result of a generalized disregard for the environment. The long-standing environmental problems have gotten worse as a consequence of the dismantling of institutionalized mechanisms of monitoring and supervision combined with an ideological mixture of permissiveness and negationism on the part of the current government. Despite arising with the support of protests against the corruption revealed in the Workers' Party governments, the public security policies of the new right-wing populist regime has not brought tranquility to the population, which finds itself caught in the cross fire between organized crime, on the one hand, and armed intervention police, on the other.

During the 1990s and 2000s, Brazil began to experience a certain prosperity accompanied by social achievements and slight democratic progress on human rights and by a public effort to seek justice. The fall of the Berlin Wall in 1989 sparked a global hope for an overcoming of the Cold War, and in Latin American countries, a path was cleared for another, different approximation to the developed world through a more equal dialogue that challenged traditional ideas of economic and cultural dependency. The challenge was directed against theories of "unequal exchange" and the Eurocentric view that delegated to Latin America a position on the global periphery destined to be always oriented toward the center of the Western world. In this manner, globalization and digital technology have not only introduced the notion of contemporaneity for a more egalitarian debate with the art and literature of the "First World," but also established, from the perspective of Brazil, a way to be included in the global financial market as a supplier of commodities and also of art and literature, which had never before enjoyed such attention and global interest.

With the new democratic constitution of 1988, followed by the achievement of economic stability during the 1990s, Brazil not only gained global political recognition but also emerged as an innovative contributor to the debates on the inconclusive legacy of modernity. Thus, the end of the twentieth century closed in light of the question of postmodernity based on a decolonial geography that was beginning to design its independence in a challenge to Western thinking. The celebration of the five hundred year anniversary of the so-called discovery of the Americas in 1992, and its coincidence with the 70-year anniversary of the Brazilian Modern Art Week, instigated the reformulation of the legacy of Brazilian and Latin American modernism for a more inclusive modernity with a positive and plural recovery of its periphery. Brazil was beginning to find its unique role in the postcolonial scenario, in which it simultaneously represented the legacy of economic underdevelopment, marked socially by its history of slavery, and by a certain vanguard of sensible experiments in popular culture. Its corporal and musical expression seemed, in the light of rereadings, to propose examples for the inclusive, multiethnic and cultural policies of the twenty-first century. Facilitated by new global circuits of digital communication and by media ubiquity, local encounters arose in new interactive spaces bringing the emergence of an anachronistic agency that allowed the updating of the past to serve as a guide for the future.

The new regional topologies were what destabilized the customary hierarchical relation between the developed "First World" and the "Third World" under development. Historical time became so complex that it challenged the very concept of nation and mainly the perspective of nation building.[1] In the

---

[1] Silviano Santiago contrasted the idea of nation-building (*formação*) with what he called the episteme of inclusion (*inserção*) ("Formação e Inserção" (literally, Formation and Insertion), *Estadão*, May 26, 2012).

1970s, economists[2] referred to Brazil as "BelIndia," a monster whose small head represented an upper "Belgian" class and whose fat body represented a poverty and deprivation comparable to that of India. At the beginning of the twenty-first century, the minister Delfim Neto opted for the image of "Enghana" to characterize the high level of public taxation, comparable to that of England, and the low level of public services, comparable to that of Ghana. Afterward,[3] under pressure due to the crisis in public security, the metaphor of "Braziliation" foresaw Brazil as the vanguard of "favelization" in the world, which was causing a situation of violence and crime that was forcing the middle and upper classes to imprison themselves in gated communities heavily protected by private security services.

In the Lula administrations from 2002 to 2010, the country defied this fate and began to dream of a place among the big shots, by achieving recognition as the fifth biggest economy in the world and a surprising jump in social mobility as a result of its income redistribution policy, its continental leadership in Latin America and its global ambition to become a member of the UN Security Council. There seemed to be no limit to the country's good fortune, as Brazil naturally earned the right to host the 2014 World Cup and 2016 Olympic Games, much earlier than the onset of the 2013 economic crisis, which along with the corruption scandals made evident the critical situation of the Workers' Party governmental policies that led the country to its worst moment of depression and unemployment since the return of democracy in 1985.

With the 2018 elections and the victory of Jair Bolsonaro, an incredible representative of a "new old Brazil" committed to the great dismantling of everything considered to be the fruit of the young democracy and even "democracy" itself, an unpleasant state of revenge and hatred when not direct violence took over the public sphere, thereby creating a never-before-seen challenge for literature. Today it is not enough to act in defense of freedom of expression against the attempts at ideological control and direct censorship, nor to defend the abstract right for art and literature to exist in the face of the ignorance of a government that only sees in them an ideological threat. At the current moment, it concerns showing the real relevance of literature in its capacity to respond to life as experienced, before being questioned, and to intervene in all possible ways, from critical revelation to affective realization.

---

[2] Edmar Lisboa Bacha. 1974. "O Rei da Belíndia" [The King of BelIndia]. PDF file available on the website of the Institute for Economic Policy Studies (Rio de Janeiro: IEPE).

[3] Braziliation, apud Michael Lind (1995).

The most recent novel by Chico Buarque de Holanda, *Essa Gente* (These people), was released on November 14, 2019 and consists of a series of diary entries by a writer named Duarte, a resident in Leblon, Rio de Janeiro, who relates how difficult it is for him to overcome writer's block and manage his personal relationships with his ex-wife, his son, his editor, his neighbors and a wide range of other typical *carioca* characters from this upper-class neighborhood. The brutalization of social relations, intolerance, violence and constant stupidity provide the general tone of the dialogues. Real and recent occurrences in the city are mixed with fiction, and the result is a portrait of the current state of affairs that is closer to a chronicle.

The chronology of the chapters, always marked by very recent dates, offers the reader the sensation of a daily blog that reconciles everyday incidents and sociopolitical events from a very recent past. Beginning on November 30, 2018 and ending on September 29, 2019, the narrative covers the fateful year of 2019 and is only interrupted by some flashbacks and letters from the past, the oldest of which is from February 12, 1999. The back cover of the novel informs the reader that the first edition was published on November 14, 2019. Thus, the supposed distance between what is described and the act of writing is radically diminished, and an effect of *simultaneity* is produced that is normally not achieved in literary fiction. It is a story about the present written "in medias res," as it occurs, and the time is neither that of the epic of grand narratives nor that of the revelatory account focused on the privileged instant of a sudden transformation. The story thus gains a hallucinatory resonance by appearing at the moment of the events in question, which is in line with the author's explicit intent to comment upon and intervene in current affairs.

To the extent that it characterizes contemporary fiction, Chico Buarque's writing tends to erase the difference between fiction and reality, the temporal distance between writing and its scene, and to exceed through its desire to intervene by fictionally interacting with real events. Everything is fiction and everything is real, not only because the context appears in some achingly real events, such as the execution of an innocent musician with 80 gunshots by the public security forces, but also because the novel is an *act* of listening to a certain tone and certain voices of Brazil today. Some fragments are messages, letters and notes that circulate among the characters. Others are brief accounts, as if they were personal records of the protagonist. The novel's ironic narrative does not try to interpret the historical logic behind the actions related and is converted into an activity that in itself is an act of storytelling as the action takes place. It thus explores the "presence of the present," the here and now and seeks its authenticity in this blatant "ontology of the present" that is contemporary to the extent that it does not try to explain the ballast of history and rejects promising any relief in the future.

Without a doubt, the contemporary in art and literature has been perceived since the turn of the century as a temporal complexity that has challenged the modern historiographic certainties of a sequential continuity in historical time that supported a whole hermeneutic universe of causes and effects. In the heated discussion of "the postmodern versus the modern," critics of modernity such as François Lyotard recognized that the "post" argument in itself arose from the modern view and therefore strictly speaking represented its genealogical defense. As a result of this type of sophism, the quarrel between the modern and postmodern camps has lost its explanatory power, and a discursive space has been opened up for the question of the contemporary.

In its colloquial sense, the contemporary only records the temporal coincidence between two phenomena, but the discussion has gained importance to the extent that the contemporary began to mean something beyond this strictly chronological argument (X happened at the same time as Y), evoking the perception of a multiplicity of coexisting times and therefore an exacerbated permeability among the conceptual boundaries of past, present and future. Nonetheless, the contemporary does not only concern an epistemological relation between a chronological time and a duration that makes it possible to pass through different levels of chronology. It also concerns, from the geopolitical perspective of globalization, local spaces (cities, neighborhoods, everyday events, private experiences, etc.) that within global spaces (the media, technology, the economy and the public sphere) establish material perspectives of temporal experiences and their simultaneous coexistence. This is how the space of the nation loses relevance and retreats in the face of the global mobility acquired as a result of circuits of approximation and interaction in restricted spaces of commerce, migration, art and culture, as well as of political resistance and utopian or alternative thinking that ignore national boundaries and often traverse the hierarchical relations of center and periphery.

Like Appadurai, who in the 1990s identified the five "scapes" in postmodern society, one witnesses today a plural density of globalized spaces that create the material conditions for the complex temporalities of the contemporary. In the 1980s, the anthropologist Johannes Fabian (1983) criticized the Western view of the "other" as backward in its development and not fully contemporary with the First World as a result of a spatiotemporal distance that he called "allochronism." For Fabian, the requirement for a critical anthropology was to demand full contemporaneity for all cultures against the "chronopolitical" tendency that perpetuated colonial inferiority. From this perspective, the contemporary as a politics of the present established a real platform of dialogue without imperial hierarchies, and in Brazil, it was translated into the experience of being recognized at the same table as a global partner. Nonetheless, even though the historian Dipesh Chakrabarty (2008) agrees with Fabian's critique of the "backwardness" of non-Western cultures, he insists on the potential for recognition of moments of an authentic "heterotemporality" in relation to the global "present" and therefore of a certain coexistence of different temporal layers.

That is how recent fiction, for example, manages to give a testimony of local spheres within the national sphere itself, in which the temporalities of the past and even of the future coexist in their historical presence. Two examples are worth mentioning in this sense, the novel *Torto Arado* (Crooked plow, 2019), by Itamar Vieira Junior, and *Verão Tardio* (Late summer, 2019) by Luiz Ruffato.

In a striking debut novel from 2018, the young Bahian author Itamar Vieira Junior manages to create a universal environment in his description of a small community in the state of Bahia. At Água Negra, a farm in the region of Chapada Diamantina, the story accompanies the sisters Bibiana and Belonísia, daughters of Zeca Chapéu Grande, a leader of the Afro-Brazilian Jaré religion practiced by the mostly black rural workers in the region. Based on ethnographic work in the region, the author recreates in narrative language the social fabric of a *quilombola* or maroon community in which slavery penetrates and is present in all of the relationships revealed. With the magic touch of a Juan Rulfo, the "time of violence" gains a transhistorical and "heterotemporal" dimension. All of a sudden, one perceives the slave society's past recover its reality and resilience in the rhythm of the narratives, in the enchanted environment, in the pacing of the story and in a material way at certain places and in certain simple objects, such as in a sharp knife that the grandmother kept and which will mark the sisters' lives.

In 2019, the Minas Gerais author Luiz Ruffato released the novel *Verão Tardio*, which reflects the failure of hopes for a fulfilling life in an exploration of the dissolution of family and community ties in Brazilian society. All of Ruffato's work explores this theme based on the story of the Zona da Mata in Minas Gerais, but this recent novel expresses a historical present that is trapped by the past and that becomes an allegory for the country. For six days, Oseias returns to Cataguazes, his hometown, and looks for his friends and family in search of some understanding of a life that now seems to be pathetically coming to a close because of a disease and also the little that is left of affective and social ties. Oseias looks for answers without recognizing the questions. He abandoned the city 40 years ago in favor of a life in São Paulo and visited it for the last time in 1995, before his mother's death. Thus, he himself is part of the dissolution, and what seems to remain is disaffection, disaggregation and guilt. Why did his sister Lígia kill herself? Oseias's melancholy and the presence of the past are superimposed on the chronological present that organizes the novel into six days in a row, and the encounters or "disencounters" on the character's path do not lead to anything but the tangled threads of what has passed. Thus, the historical present only reflects a certain past that does not pass, or else it would foreclose any possibility of mourning and overcoming and convert the present into a macabre and sick repetition of past traumas.

The odyssey of Oseias (an anagram?) offers a sinister image of a past that not only "does not pass" but also hinders and obstructs the present as a path and a possibility. Thus, the ballast of the past is not unburdened, and unlike Ulysses, Oseias is not truly "recognized" upon his return to Ithaca nor is his past epically redeemed. Instead of an understanding of his own story, melancholy for Oseias is converted into a deep sadness for the missed opportunities of a life that was not lived. Thus, Ruffato's novel becomes a politically allegorical mirror of a present that is negatively bound by the mistakes committed, in contrast to *Torto Arado*, by Itamar Vieira Junior, in which the presence of the past is a resource for resistance and survival, a historical and cultural diversity that has been reencountered.

Contemporary authoritarianism aims to rewrite history and erase the lessons learned from the errors of past while negating and ignoring the destruction of the future. To live in the present has become a dictatorship of ideological ignorance in which the pillars of freedom are dismantled and the walls of censorship are erected in the name of the interests of power and greed.

BIBLIOGRAPHY

Agamben, Giorgio. 1993. *Infancy and History: The Destruction of Experience*. Translated by Liz Heron. London: Verso.

———. 2009. *What Is an Apparatus? And Other Essays*. Translated by David Kishik and Stefan Pedatella. Stanford, CA: Stanford University Press.

———. 2005. *The Time That Remains: A Commentary on the Letter to the Romans*. Translated by Patricia Dailey. Palo Alto, CA: Stanford University Press.

Appadurai, A. 1990. "Disjuncture and Difference in the Global Cultural Economy." *Public Culture* 2, no. 1: 1–24.

Aquino, Marçal. 2005. *Eu receberia as piores notícias de seus lindos lábios*. São Paulo: Companhia das Letras.

Arendt, Hannah. 2005. *The Promise of Politics*. Edited by Jerome Kohn. New York: Schocken Books.

Assis, Machado de. 2018. "Reflections on Brazilian Literature at the Present Moment: The National Instinct." Translated by Robert Patrick Newcomb. *Brasil/Brazil* 26, no. 47: 85–101.

Auerbach, Erich. 2003. *Mimesis: The Representation of Reality in Western Thought*. Princeton, NJ: Princeton University Press.

Austin, J. L. 1962. *How to Do Things with Words: The William James Lectures Delivered at Harvard University in 1955*. Edited by James O. Urmson. Oxford: Oxford University Press.

Baker, Nicholas. 1993. *Vox*. New York: Vintage Books.

———. 1994. *The Fermata*. New York: Vintage Books.

Badiou, Alain. 2004. *Handbook of Inaesthetics*. Translated by Alberto Toscano. Stanford, CA: Stanford University Press.

Ballard, J. G. 1995. *Crash*. London. Verso.

Barthes, Roland. 1981. *Camera Lucida: Reflections on Photography*. Translated by Richard Howard. New York: Hill and Wang.

———. 1986. *The Rustle of Language*. Translated by Richard Howard. Berkeley: University of California Press.

Baudrillard, Jean. 1993. *Symbolic Exchange and Death (Published in association with Theory, Culture & Society)*. Translated by Lain Hamilton Grant. London: Sage.

Benveniste, E. [1966] 1973. "Active and Middle Voice in the Verb." In *Problems in General Linguistics*. Translated by Mary Elizabeth Meek, 145–51. Coral Gables, FL: University of Miami Press.

Berg, Gretchen. 1967. "Andy: My True Story." *Los Angeles Free Press*, March 17, p. 3.

Bernhard, Thomas. 2006. *Gathering Evidence: A Memoir*. Translated by David McLintock. New York: Vintage Books.

Blanchot, Maurice. 1982. *The Space of Literature*. Translated by Ann Smock. London: University of Nebraska Press.
Booth, Wayne C. 1961. *The Rhetoric of Fiction*. Chicago: University of Chicago Press.
Bolaño, Roberto. 2013. *Entre parentesis*. Barccelona: Anagrama.
Brooks, Peter. 2005. *Realist Vision*. New Haven, CT: Yale University Press.
Bürger, Peter. 1984. *Theory of the Avant-Garde (Theory and History of Literature)*. Minneapolis: University of Minnesota Press.
Carvalho, Bernardo. 2003. *Mongólia*. São Paulo: Companhia das Letras.
———. 2007. *O Céu se põe em São Paulo*. São Paulo: Companhia das Letras.
———. 2009. *Filho da Mãe* São Paulo: Companhia das Letras.
Buarque de Holanda, Chico. 2009. *Leite derramado*. São Paulo: Companhia das Letras.
———. 2012. *Spilt Milk*. Translated by Allison Entrekin. London: Atlantic Books.
———. 2014. *My German Brother*. Translated by Alison Entrekin. New York: Picador.
———. 2019. *Essa Gente*. São Paulo: Companhia das Letras.
Certeau, Michel de. [1980] 1984. *The Practice of Everyday Life*. Translated by Steven F. Rendall. Berkeley: University of California Press.
Chakrabarty, D. 2008. *Provincializing Europe: Postcolonial Thought and Historical Difference*. Princeton, NJ: Princeton University Press.
Cesar, Ana Cristina. 2013. *Poética*. São Paulo: Companhia das Letras.
———. 2018. *At Your Feet*. Translated by Brenda Hillman, edited by Katrina Dodson (Free Verse Editions) New York: Parlor Press.
Chatwin, Bruce. 1990. *What Am I Doing Here*. London: Penguin Books.
Coelho, Paulo. 2014. *The Alchemist*. Translated by Allan R. Clarke. New York: HarperOne.
———. 2016. *The Spy*. Translated by Zoë Perry. New York: Alfred A. Knopf.
Coelho, Teixeira. 2006. *História natural da ditadura*. São Paulo: Iluminuras.
Conde, Miguel. 2018. "Na travessia, ele inventou o próprio ritmo" [On the journey, he invented his own rhythm]. http://www.suplementopernambuco.com.br/edições-anteriores/72-resenha/2071-na-travessia,-ele-inventou-o-próprio-ritmo.html. Accessed September 1, 2020.
Cuenca, J. P. 2016. *Descobri que estava morto*. São Paulo: Planeta do Brasil.
Dalcastagnè, Regina. 2013. *Literatura brasileira contemporânea: um território contestado*. Rio de Janeiro: Editora da Universidade do Estado do Rio de Janeiro.
Derrida, J. [1967] 2016. *Of Grammatology*. Translated by Gayatri Chakravorty Spivak and introduction by Judith Butler. Baltimore: John Hopkins Press.
———. [1972] 1982. *Margins of Philosophy*. Translated by Alan Bass. Chicago: University of Chicago Press.
Drummond de Andrade, Carlos. 2012. *Claro Enigma*. São Paulo: Companhia das Letras.
Drummond, Maria Clara. 2015. *A realidade devia ser proibida*. São Paulo: Companhia das Letras.
Elkins, James. 2013. *Beyond the Aesthetic and the Anti-Aesthetic*. Philadelphia: Penn State University Press.
Ellis, Bret Easton. 1985. *Less Than Zero*. New York: Simon & Schuster.
———. 1991. *American Psyco*. New York: Vintage Books.
Fabian, J. 1983. *Time and the Other. How Anthropology Makes Its Object*. New York: Columbia University Press.
Felman, Shoshana, and Dori Laub. 1991. *Testimony: Crises of Witnessing in Literature, Psychoanalysis, and History*. London: Routledge.

Ferraris, M. 2012. *Documentality: Why It Is Necessary to Leave Traces.* New York: Fordham University Press.
Fonseca, Rubem. 1990. *Agosto.* São Paulo: Companhia das Letras.
Foster, Hal. 1983. *The Anti-Aesthetic. Essays on Postmodern Culture.* Port Bay: Bay Press.
———. 1994. *The Return of the Real.* Cambridge, MA: MIT Press.
———. 1995. *Compulsive Beauty.* Cambridge, MA: MIT Press.
———. 1996. "Death in America." *October* 75 (Winter): 36–59.
Foucault, Michel. 2002. *The Order of Things: An Archaeology of the Human Sciences.* New York: Routledge.
———. 1999. "*The Meaning and Evolution of the Word 'Parrhesia': Discourse & Truth, Problematization of Parrhesia.*" Six lectures given by Michel Foucault at the University of California at Berkeley, October–November 1983. https://foucault.info/parrhesia/foucault.DT1.wordParrhesia.en/. Accessed September 3, 2020.
Freire, Marcelino. 2013. *Nossos Ossos.* Record. Rio de Janeiro
Fúks, Julián. 2019. *Resistance.* Translated by Daniel Hahn. Edingburg: Charco Press.
Fux, Jacques. 2015. *Brochadas: Confissões sexuais de um jovem escritor.* Rio de Janeiro: Rocco.
Galera, Daniel. 2001. *Dentes Guardados.* Porto Alegre: Livros do Mal.
———. 2003. *Até o Dia em que o Cão Morreu.* Porto Alegre: Livros do Mal.
———. 2006. *Mãos de Cavalo.* São Paulo: Companhia das Letras.
———. 2008. *Cordilheira.* São Paulo: Companhia das Letras.
———. 2012. *Barba ensopada de sangue.* São Paulo: Companhia das Letras.
———. 2015. *Blood-Drenched Beard.* Translated by Alison Entrekin. New York: Penguin Books.
Groys, B. 2010. *Going Public.* Berlin. Sternberg Press.
Heller, Agnes. [1970] 1984. *Everyday Life.* London: Routledge & Kegan Paul.
Jackson, Kenneth David. 2008. "A Statesman in the Academy: Joaquim Nabuco at Yale." *Estudos Avançados* 22, no. 62: 335–49. http://www.scielo.br/pdf/ea/v22n62/en_a22v2262.pdf. Accessed September 1, 2020.
Izhaki, Flávio. 2013. *Amanhã não tem ninguém.* Rio de Janeiro: Rocco.
———. 2016. *Tentativas de capturar o ar.* Rio de Janeiro: Rocco.
Jameson, Fredric. 2013. *The Antinomies of Realism.* London: Verso.
Jesus, Carolina Maria de. [1962] 2003. *Child of the Dark: The Diary of Carolina Maria De Jesus.* Translated by David St. Clair. New York: Mass Market Paperback.
Kant, Immanuel. 2008. *Zum ewigen Frieden und andere Schriften*, Frankfurt: Fischer.
Keenan, Thomas, and Eyal Weizman. 2012. *Mengele's Skull—The Advent of a Forensic Aesthetics.* Berlin: Sternberg Press/Portikus.
Kucinski, Bernardo. 2011. *K: Relato de uma busca.* São Paulo: Companhia das Letras.
———. 2013. *K: Report of a Search.* Translated by Sue Branford. London: Latin American Bureau.
Knausgaard, Karl. [2009] 2012. *My Struggle.* Translated by Don Bartlett. New York: Archipelago.
Kundera, Milan. 2003. *The Art of the Novel.* New York: Harper.
Lacan, Jacques. 1998. "Of the Gaze as Objet Petit a." In *The Seminar of Jacques Lacan, Book XI: The Four Fundamental Concepts of Psychoanalysis.* Edited by Jacques-Alain Miller, 67–122. New York: Norton.
Laddaga, R. 2011. *Estética da emergência: a formação de outra cultura das artes.* São Paulo. Martins Fontes.
Laub, Michel. 2013. *A Poison Apple.* Translated by Daniel Hahn. London: Harwill Secker.

———. 2014. *Diary of the Fall*. Translated by Margaret Jull Costa. London: Harwill Secker.
Lefebvre, Henri. [1968] 2016. *Everyday Life in the Modern World*. London: Bloomsbury.
Leiris, Michel. 1984. *Manhood: A Journey from Childhood into the Fierce Order of Virility*. Translated by Richard Howard. Chicago: University of Chicago Press.
Leminski, Paulo. 2013. *Toda poesia*. São Paulo: Companhia das Letras.
Leones, André de. 2011. *Dentes negros*. Rio de Janeiro: Rocco.
Lima, Luiz Costa. 2011. "No Novo Milênio: Um novo romance?" *Suplemento Trimestral da Ciência Hoje*. 5 (2. maio).
Lind, Michael. 1995. *The Next American Nation: The New Nationalism and the Fourth American Revolution*. New York: Free Press.
Lins, Paulo. 1997a. *Cidade de Deus*. São Paulo: Companhia das Letras.
———. 1997b. *City of God*. Translated by Alison Entrekin. New York: Black Cat.
———. 2012. *Desde que o samba é samba*. São Paulo: Planeta.
Lisias, Ricardo. 2012. *O céu dos suicidas*. Rio de Janeiro: Alfaguara.
———. 2013. *Divórcio*. Rio de Janeiro: Alfaguara.
———. 2014. *Delegado Tobias 1–5*. e-galáxia.
———. 2016. *A vista particular*. Rio de Janeiro: Alfaguara.
———. 2017. *Diário da cadeia por Eduardo Cunha (Pseudónimo)*. Rio de Janeiro: Record.
Ludmer, Josefina. 2007. "Literaturas postautónomas." *Ciberletras—Revista de crítica literaria y de cultura 17*. http://www.lehman.cuny.edu/ciberletras/v17/ludmer.htm. Accessed September 1, 2020.
———. 2010a. *Aquí América Latina: una especulación*. Buenos Aires: Eterna Cadencias.
———. 2010b. "Notas para Literaturas Posautónomas III." *Wordpress*, July 31, 2010. https://josefinaludmer.wordpress.com/2010/07/31/notas-para-literaturas-posautonomas-iii/. Accessed September 1, 2020.
Luhmann, Niklas. 1992. *Beobachtungen der Moderne*. Opladen: Westdeutscher Verlag.
Lukács, Georg. 1970. *Writer & Critic and Other Essays*. Edited and translated by Arthur D. Kahn. New York: Merlin Press.
Lyotard, Jean-François. 1988. *Peregrinations: Law, Form, Event*. Oxford: Columbia University Press.
———. 1991a. *The Inhuman: Reflections on Time*. Translated by Geoffrey Bennington and Rachel Bowlby. Cambridge: Polity Press.
———. 1991b. "The Sublime and the Avant-Garde". In *The Inhuman: Reflections on Time*. Translated by Geoffrey Bennington and Rachel Bowlby, 89–108. Cambridge: Polity Press.
Martins, Giovani. 2018. *O Sol na Cabeça*. São Paulo: Companhia das Letras.
Massumi, Brian. 1995. "The Autonomy of Affect." Cultural Critique (The Politics of Systems and Environments, Part II), no. 31 (Autumn): 83–109.
———. 2002. *Parables for the Virtual: Movement, Affect, Sensation*. Durham, NC: Duke University Press.
Melo, Patricia. 1997. *The Killer*. Translated by Clifford E. Landers. New York: Ecco.
Miranda, Ana. 1989. *Boca do inferno*. São Paulo: Companhia das Letras.
Mondzain, Marie-José. 2015. *L'image peut-elle tuer?*. Paris: Bayard Culture.
Morais, Reinaldo. 2011. *Pornopopéia*. Rio de Janeiro: Objetiva.
Moretti, Franco. 1999. *Atlas of the European Novel 1800–1900*. London: Verso.
———. 2000. "Conjectures on World Literature." *New Left Review 1* (January–February). https://newleftreview.org/issues/II1/articles/franco-moretti-conjectures-on-world-literature. Accessed September 1, 2020.
Mussa, Alberto. 2011. *O senhor do lado esquerdo*. Rio de Janeiro: Record.

———. 2013. *The Mystery of Rio*, Translated by Alex Ladd. New York: Europa Editions.
Noll, João Gilberto. [2002] 2004. *Berkeley em Bellagio*. São Paulo: Frances.
———. [1996] 2008. *A Céu Aberto*. Rio de Janeiro: Record.
———. [1993] 2013. *Harmada*. Rio de Janeiro: Record.
———. [2004] 2014. *Lorde*. Rio de Janeiro: Record.
Oliveira, Raquel de. 2015. *A Número Um*. Rio de Janeiro: Laya Brasil.
Pécora, Alcir. 2015. "Apolítica, uma literatura de segundo grau." *Sibila: Revista de poesia e crítica literária*, April 14, 2015. https://sibila.com.br/critica/apolitica-uma-literatura-de-segundo-grau/11557. Accessed September 1, 2020.
Perniola, Mario. 2013. *20th Century Aesthetics: Towards a Theory of Feeling*. London: A&C Black.
Porto, Alexandre Vidal. 2014. *Sergio Y. Vai à América*. São Paulo: Companhia das Letras.
———. 2019. *Cloro*. São Paulo: Companhia das Letras.
Rancière, Jacques. 2004a. *Malaise dans l'esthétique*. Paris: Galilée.
———. 2004b. *The Flesh of Words: The Politics of Writing*. Translated by Charlotte Mandell. Stanford, CA: Stanford University Press.
———. 2009. "The Reality Effect and the Politics of Fiction." ICI Berlin Institute for Cultural Inquiry. https://www.ici-berlin.org/events/jacques-ranciere/. Accessed September 1, 2020.
———. 2010. *Chronicles of Consensual Times*. Translated by Steven Corcoran. London: Continuum.
———. 2011. *The Politics of Aesthetics: The Distribution of the Sensible*. Translated by Gabriel Rockhill. New York: Continuum.
Ribeiro, Djamila. 2017. *O que é lugar de fala?* Belo Horizonte: Letramento.
Ribeiro, João Ubaldo. 1999. *Casa dos Budas Ditosos*. Rio de Janeiro: Objetiva.
———. [1984] 2008. *Viva o povo brasileiro*. Rio de Janeiro: Alfaguara.
Ruffato, Luiz. 1998. *Histórias de remorsos e rancores*. São Paulo: Boitempo Editorial.
———. 2000. *Os sobreviventes*. São Paulo: Boitempo Editorial.
———. 2009. *Estive em Lisboa e lembrei de você*. São Paulo: Companhia das Letras.
———. 2013. *Eram muitos cavalos*. São Paulo: Companhia das Letras.
———. 2014a. *Flores artificiais*. São Paulo: Companhia das Letras.
———. 2014b. *There Were Many Horses*. Translated by Anthony Doyle. New York: Amazon Crossing.
———. 2016a. *Inferno provisório*. São Paulo: Companhia das Letras.
———. [2007] 2016b. *De mim já nem se lembra*. São Paulo: Companhia das Letras.
———. 2019. *Verão Tardio*. São Paulo: Companhia das Letras.
Saavedra, Carola. 2007. *Toda Terça*. São Paulo: Companhia das Letras.
Sant'Anna, André. 2006. *O paraíso é bem bacana*. São Paulo: Companhia das Letras.
———. 2014. *O Brasil é Bom*. São Paulo: Companhia das Letras.
Santiago, Silviano. [1984] 1989. "Prosa literária atual no Brasil." In *Nas Malhas das Letras*, 24–37. São Paulo: Companhia das Letras.
———1990. "A lei do mercado." *Isto é/Senhor*, São Paulo, January 3.
———. 1996. "Atração do mundo: políticas de identidade e de globalização na moderna cultura brasileira." *Gragoatá* 1, no. 1: 31–54.
———. [1972] 2001a. "Latin American Discourse: The Space In-Between." In *The Space In-Between: Essays on Latin American Culture*. Edited by Ana Lúcia Gazzola, with an introduction by Ana Lúcia Gazzola and Wander Melo Miranda, translated by Tom Burns, Ana Lúcia Gazzola and Gareth Williams, 25–39. Durham, NC: Duke University Press.

———. [1981] 2001b. "Universality in Spite of Dependency." In *The Space In-Between: Essays on Latin American Culture*. Edited by Ana Lúcia Gazzola, with an introduction by Ana Lúcia Gazzola and Wander Melo Miranda, translated by Tom Burns, Ana Lúcia Gazzola and Gareth Williams, 53–63. Durham, NC: Duke University Press.

———. 2003. "Outubro Retalhado." *Folha de São Paulo*, November 16. https://www1.folha.uol.com.br/fsp/mais/fs1611200304.htm. Accessed September 1, 2020.

———. 2004. *O falso mentiroso*. Rio de Janeiro: Rocco.

———. 2005. *Histórias mal contadas*. Rio de Janeiro: Rocco.

———. 2008. *Heranças*. Rio de Janeiro: Rocco.

———. 2012. "Formação e Inserção." *Estadão*, May 26.

Schøllhammer, Karl Erik. 2012. "Realismo afetivo: evocar realismo além da representação". *Estudos de Literatura Brasileira Contemp*orânea, no. 39 (January–June). http://dx.doi.org/10.1590/S2316-40182012000100008. Accessed September 1, 2020.

———. 2015a. "A história natural da ditadura". *Lua Nova* 96: 39–54.

———. 2015b "O pacto renovado com a história—o realismo contemporâneo brasileiro." *Ciência Hoje*, 288.

———. 2016a. "A literatura brasileira contemporânea na perspectiva mundial." In *Literatura e Artes na Crítica Contemporânea*. Edited by Heidrun Krieger Olinto, Karl Erik Schøllhammer and Mariana Maia Simoni, 159–68. Rio de Janeiro: Editora PUC-Rio.

———. 2016b. "Do realismo ao pós-realismo." *Scripta* 20, no. 39: 14–21.

———. 2016c. "Um Mundo de papel—reflexões sobre o Realismo de Luiz Ruffato." *Alea-Estudos Neolatinos* 18, no. 2: 232–42.

———. 2017a. "A volta vitoriosa do eu na narrativa contemporânea." In *Impasses do narrador e da narrativa*. Edited by Maria Rosa Duarte; Maria José Palo. São Paulo: EDUC.

———. 2017b. "Inventário do real." In *Atores em Cena: O público e o privado na literatura brasileira contemporânea*. Edited by Ángela Maria Dias and Sterfania Chiarelli, 233–45. Rio de Janeiro: Oficina Raquel.

Scott, Paulo. 2001. *Histórias curtas para domesticar as paixões dos anjos e atenuar o sofrimento dos monstrous*. Porto Alegre: Sulina.

———. 2005. *Voléteis*. Rio de Janeiro: Objetiva.

———. 2007. *Ainda orangotangos*. São Paulo: Bertrand.

———. 2011a. *Nowhere People*. Translated by Daniel Hahn. London: And Other Stories.

———. 2011b. *Habitante Irreal*. Rio de Janeiro: Alfaguara.

Sebald, Winfried Georg. 1998. *The Rings of Saturn*. London: New Directions.

———. 2001. *On the Natural History of Destruction*. Translated by Anthea Bell. New York: Random House.

Seltzer, Mark. 1995. "Serial Killers (II): The Pathological Public Sphere." *Critical Inquiry* 22, no. 1 (Autumn): 122–49.

———. 1998. *Serial Killer: Death and Life in America's Wound Culture*. London: Routledge.

Schwarz, Roberto. 1988. "Brazilian Culture: Nationalism by Elimination." *New Left Review* 1 (January–February), 167.

———. 1992. *Misplaced Ideas: Essays on Brazilian Culture*. (Critical Studies in Latin American Culture). New York: Verso.

Siskind, Mariano. 2014. *Cosmopolitan Desires—Global Modernity and World Literature in Latin America*. Chicago: Northwestern University Press.

Soares, Jô e Matinaz Suzuki. 2017. *O Livro de Jô*. São Paulo: Companhia das Letras.

Souza, Eneida Maria de. 2002. *Crítica cult*. Belo Horizonte: Editora UFMG.

Teixeira de Vasconcelos, A. A. 1863. *Viagens na terra alheia, de Paris a Madrid*. Lisboa: Typographia do Futuro.

Tezza, Cristovão. 2013. *Eternal Son*. Translated by Alison Entrekin. Melbourne: Scribe Publications.

Thrift, Nigel. 2007. *Non-Representational Theory: Space, Politics, Affect*. London: Routledge.

Vieira Junior, Itamar. 2019. *Torto Arado*. São Paulo: Todavia.

Watt, Ian. 1957. *The Rise of the Novel: Studies in Defoe, Richardson, and Fielding*. Berkeley: University of California Press.

Žižek, Slavoj. 2004. "The Parallax View." *New Left Review* 25 (January–February).

INDEX

After Nature 23
Agamben, Giorgio 4–6, 17, 82, 103
age of testimony 21–22
Agosto (Fonseca) 11
Alchemist, The (Coelho) 66
Allende, Isabel 61
Alltagsgeschichte 47
Almeida, Marco Rodrigo 25
Alves, Francisco 10
Amado, Jorge 11, 64, 65
Amanhã não tem ninguém (Izhaki) 32
American Psycho (Ellis) 79
Amores Expressos (Love Express) project 2, 68, 94
anachronism 5–6, 93
Anti-Aesthetic: Essays on Postmodern Culture (Foster) 101
anti-aesthetics 101–6
antidiscipline, network of 47
Aquino, Marçal 11
Argentinian dictatorship 20
art, regime of 38–39
   aesthetic 39
   ethical 38–39
   poetic 39
Até o Dia em que o Cão Morreu (Until the day the dog died; Galera) 68
Atlas of the European Novel (Moretti) 87
At Your Feet (Cesar) 65
Auerbach, Erich 26, 39, 41, 46–48
authoritarianism 19–20
(auto)biography 7–8, 32–34, 54, 63, 72, 81
autofiction 25, 71–84
autonomy 39
avant-garde 31, 107

Badiou, Alain 30
Baker, Nicholson 79
Bandeira, Manuel 10
Bar Apolo 10
Barcellos, Caco 65
Barcelos, Alcebíades 10
Barthes, Roland 4–5, 26, 29, 39, 47–48, 77–78
Baudrillard, Jean 55
Benjamin, Walter 6–7, 15, 20–21, 23, 47–48, 78
Berkeley em Bellagio (Berkeley in Bellagio; Noll) 94
Bernhard, Thomas 79
Blanchot, Maurice 72
Blood-Drenched Beard (Galera) 68–70
Boca do Inferno (Mouth of hell; Miranda) 11, 63
Bolaño, Roberto 61–62, 64
Bolsonaro, Jair 111
Bonassi, Fernando 4
Booth, Wayne C. 72
Borges, Jorge Luis 52
BR3: Brasilândia—Brasília—Brasiléia 96
Brasilândia 96–97
Brasiléia 96–97
Brazilian literature
   (auto)biography 7–8, 32–34, 54, 63, 72, 81
   challenges 8, 101–10
   contemporary in 1–24, 111–17
   criticism 87–99
   dictatorship, natural history of 19–24
   literary fiction *vs.* general fiction 12
   and market 3, 61–70
   nineteenth-century 25
   pact with history 8–19
   presentification 2–3, 72–73, 75–76

Brazilian literature (cont.)
  private products 7–8
  realism in 8, 25–34
  role 3
  social commitment 3–4
  and society 3–4
  trauma of history 6–8, 29–30, 50–51
  twentieth-century 8–9
  twenty-first century 9
  voice 31–32
  Weltliteratur (world literature) and 87–99
Breton, André 49
Brochadas (Impotence; Fux) 71, 79
Brown, Dan 63
Brown, Thomas 23
Buarque, Chico 65, 114

Café do Compadre 10
Calle, Sophie 81
Camera Lucida: Reflections on Photography (Barthes) 48
Candido, Antonio 89
Capão pecado (Capão sin; Ferréz) 29
Carvalho, Bernardo 75, 83, 94
Casa dos Budas Ditosos (House of the fortunate Buddhas; Ribeiro) 63
Casa entre vertebras (Peres) 18
Castro, Ruy 65
Célio, José 36
Cesar, Ana Cristina 65
César, Joana 73–75
Céu Aberto (Open sky; Noll) 94
Chakrabarty, Dipesh 115–16
Chatwin, Bruce 79
Ciata, Tia 10
City of God (Lins) 9, 10–11, 29, 54
Claro Enigma (Clear enigma; de Andrade) 65
Cobain, Kurt 14
Coelho, Paulo 64–67
Coelho, Teixeira 20, 22–23
Companhia das Letras 9, 63
Conde, Miguel 59
"Conjectures on World Literature" 88
contemporary literature 1–24. *See also* Brazilian literature
contemporary writing, self in 71–84
Cordilheira (Mountain range; Galera) 68–69

Cuenca, João Paulo 75
Cury, Augusto 64
cybernetic privacy 45

Das Unheimliche (Freud) 49
Datrino, José 73
de Andrade, Carlos Drummond 65
de Andrade, Mário 10
de Andrade, Oswald 89
de Assis, Machado 25
Death in America (Warhol) 30
de Certeau, Michel 47
de Holanda, Chico Buarque 11, 54, 79, 114
Deixa Falar 10
de Jesus, Carolina Maria 57
Delcastagnè, Regina 53–54
"*Delegado Tobias*" (Sheriff Tobias) 84
de Leones, André 18
Deleuze, Gilles 109
De mim já nem se lembra (They No Longer Remember Me) 35–36
democratization 39
Dentes Guardados (Stored teeth; Galera) 68
Dentes negros (de Leones) 18
de Oliveira, Raquel 54, 58
Derrida, Jacques 77
de Sade, Marquis 26
Descobri que estava morto (Cuenca) 75
Desde que o samba é samba (Lins) 9–10
de Souza, Eneida Maria 89
de Souza Sampaio, Sérgio 36
"*Diário da Cadeia*" (Jail Diary) 84
Diary of a Magus, The 65
Diary of the Fall (Laub) 14, 79
Diathesis 77
dictatorship, natural history of 19–24
Dilthey, Wilhelm 47
Divórcio (Divorce; Lísias) 78, 83–84
documentality 73
dos Prazeres, Heitor 10
Drummond, Maria Clara 79

Eichmann trial in Jerusalem 16
Eleven Minutes (Coelho) 66–67
Elkins, James 102
Ellis, Bret Easton 79
Enghana 113

enunciandum (enunciating) 81
Erfahrung 47
Erlebnis 47
Essa Gente (These people; de Holanda) 114
Estive em Lisboa e lembrei devocé (I Was in Lisbon and Was Reminded of You) 35–36, 44
Eternal Son, The (Tezza) 71
Everyday Life (Heller) 47
Everyday Life in the Modern World (Lefebvre) 47

Fabian, Johannes 115
feeling 103
Felman, Shoshana 21
Fernandes, Sílvio 10
Ferrari, León 23
Ferraris, Maurizio 73–5
Filho da Mãe (Son of a mother; Carvalho) 94
Finetto, Dório 36–37, 43–4
first-person narrator 71–84
First World 115
Flores artificiais 36, 44
FLUPP Literary Festival project 54
Fonseca, Rubem 11, 63
Foster, Hal 15, 29–30, 49–50, 101
Foucault, Michel 26, 47, 81–83
Freire, Marcelino 4, 97
Fuks, Julián 71
Fux, Jacques 71

Galera, Daniel 9, 68–70
Garcia-Roza, Luiz Alfredo 63
Garden of Cyrus (Brown) 23
Gathering Evidence 79
Gazzola, Regina 37
Goiás 18
Goodman, Nelson 103
Gothic literature 26
Grande, Zeca Chapéu 116
Groys, Boris 84
Guattari, Félix 109
Gumbrecht, Hans Ulrich 13

Habermas, Jürgen 103
Hari, Mata 66–67
Harmada (Noll) 94

Heller, Agnes 47
História natural da ditadura (Coelho) 20
Histórias de remorsos e rancores 40
Histórias mal contadas (Badly told stories) 79
Homer's epic 26, 46

Ilibagiza, Immaculée 14
Ilustríssima 25
indexical realism 38
Infancy and History 5–6
Inferno provisório (Temporary hell; Ruffato) 29, 35, 63
inscription, theory of 73–74
insensible sensation 30
intentionality 73
Izhaki, Flávio 32–33

Jabor, Arnaldo 65
Jameson, Fredric 27–28, 31, 48–49
Joyce, James 46
Junior, Itamar Vieira 116

kairos 5
Kant, Immanuel 84, 90, 98–99, 103–8
Karatani, Kojin 98
Keenan, Thomas 16
Killer, The (Melo) 63
Kindness Prophet, The 73
Knausgaard, Karl 79
knowledge aesthetics 103
kronos 5
Kucinski, Bernardo 19–21
Kundera, Milan 12

Lacan, Jacques 29
Laddaga, Reinaldo 84
Latin America 112–13
Laub, Dori 21
Laub, Michel 14, 79
Law of Markets 62
Lebensphilosophie 47
Lefebvre, Henry 47
Leminski, Paulo 65
Less Than Zero (Ellis) 79
Lima, Luiz Costa 98
Lins, Paulo 9–11, 57
Lísias, Ricardo 75, 78
Literatura ou Morte (Literature or death) 63

Livros do Mal 9
Livros do Mal (Books of Evil) 68
Lorde (Noll) 94
Ludmer, Josefina 3, 6, 45–46, 55–57, 77, 79–80
Luhmann, Niklas 97–98
Lyotard, François 115
Lyotard, Jean-François 13, 103, 107–10

MacLeod, Rudolf John 66
Madame Bovary (Flaubert) 26, 39–40, 54–55
Malaise dans l'esthétique (Rancière) 52–3
malandroism 10
market, Brazilian literature 3, 61–70
Martins, Giovani 54, 58–59
Massumi, Brian 109–10
McLuhan, Marshall 103
Meirelles, Fernando 9
Melo, Patrícia 63
Mengele, Josef 16–17
metaliterariness 36
Miranda, Ana 11, 63
modernity 38–41
Mondzain, Jean-Marie 22
Mongólia (Carvalho) 94
Moraes, Fernando 65
Morais, Reinaldo 11, 79
Moretti, Franco 87–8
Mussa, Alberto 13
My German Brother (Buarque) 65
Mystery of Rio, The (Mussa) 13
My Struggle (Knausgaard) 79

Nabuco, Joaquim 44, 89
nachträglichkeit 15
national instinct 25
neorealisms 42
Neruda, Pablo 61
Neto, Delfim 113
network of antidiscipline 47
Noll, João Gilberto 78, 94
nonrepresentational 59
Nosotros no sabíamos 23
Nossos Ossos (Our bones; Freire) 97
Notes from the Underground (Dostoyevsky) 78
novel, globalization of 44
novelistic realism 39–40
Nowhere People (Scott) 9, 11–12, 29, 79

Número Um, A (The number one; de Oliveira) 54
Nuremberg trials 16

O céu dos suicidas (Suicide sky; Lísias) 78
O Céu se põe em São Paulo (The sun sets in São Paulo; Carvalho) 94
O falso mentiroso (The fake liar) 79
Old Testament 26, 39, 46
O Livro de Jô (The book of Jô; Soares) 63
On the Natural History of Destruction 23
O paraíso é bem bacana (Paradise is really cool; Sant'Anna) 49–50, 95
Operation Mosaic II 58
Oseias 117
O Sol na Cabeça (The sun overhead; Martins) 54
osteobiography 17

Pellizari, Daniel 9
Pellizzari, Daniel 68
Pereira, Alexandre 32
Peres, Wesley 18
performatives, theory of 73
Perniola, Mario 102–4
Pilla, Guilherme 68
Plenos Pecados (Sheer sins) 63
Poetics (Aristotle) 41
Poison Apple, A (Laub) 14, 79
Pop movement 50
Pornopopeia (Morais) 79
Portbou 20
Porto, Alexandre Vidal 94
Portugal 44
post-autonomous literatures 45–46
postautonomy 53–59, 82
Potere Operario 20
Practice of Everyday Life, The (de Certeau) 47
pragmatic aesthetics 103
presentification 2, 13, 72–73, 75–76
private products 7–8
prosopopeia 22
punctum 29, 48

quilombola 116

Ramirez, Lívia 18
Ramos, Graciliano 27

INDEX

Rancière, Jacques 26, 30, 38–41, 48, 52–55, 57, 81–82, 106–7
Rascal, Antônio 32
realidade devia ser proibida, A (Reality should be prohibited; Drummond) 79
realisms 8, 25–34
  aesthetic regime and 30, 39–42
  autonomy and 39, 48–49
  definitions 26–7
  in everyday life 44–53
  genealogy 27
  historical boundaries/limits and 27–28, 39
  as historical movement 30
  indexical 38
  Ludmer's perspective on 45–46
  and modernism 26–27
  novelistic 39–40
  to post-realism 28–34
  reflections on 35–59
  representation *vs.* reality 50
  role and status of 26–27
  of Ruffato, Luiz 35–59
  social 29
  speculative 56, 59
  traumatic 29–30, 50–51
  urban 27
  views on 26
  violence as 26, 50–51
  visual and textual representation 30–34
  in Western literature 39
realityfiction 3, 45–46, 56–57
récit 28
register 74
Republic (Plato) 41
Resistance (Fuks) 71
Return of the Real, The (Foster) 29
Ribeiro, Djamila 57
Ribeiro, João Ubaldo 11, 63
Rings of Saturn, The (Sebald) 23, 79
Rorty, Richard 103
Rosa, João Guimarães 27
Rossi, Padre Marcelo 64
Ruffato, Luiz 4, 11, 29, 116
  everyday life, electronic media in mediation of 44–53
  Histórias de remorsos e rancores 40

historical realism 41–42
Os sobreviventes 40
postautonomy, notes on 53–59
realism, reflection on 35–59
writings approaches 40

Saavedra, Carola 51, 53
Salles, João Moreira 54
Santana, Ivan 63
Sant'Anna, André 49–50, 95
Santiago, Silviano 11, 62, 79, 89
Schwarz, Roberto 9, 88–89
Scott, Paulo 9, 11–12, 29, 79
Searle, John 73, 75
Sebald, Winfried Georg 23
self-fiction 84
self-writing 3, 25, 71–84
Seltzer, Mark 14, 51
Shape of Bones, The (Galera) 68–69
Sherman, Cindy 81
Silva, Ismael 10
Simpatia pelo Demônio (Sympathy for the devil; Carvalho) 75, 83
Snow, Clyde 17
Soares, Jô 63
social realism 50
social reality, theory of 75
speculative realism 56, 59
speech acts, theory of 73
Spilt Milk (de Hollanda) 79
Spy, The (Coelho) 66–67
studium 48
Sur 20

Teitelboim, Volodio 61
Tentativas de capturar o ar (Izhaki) 32–33
Teoria da tristeza 20
Terron, Joca Reiners 9
Tezza, Cristóvão 71
There Were Many Horses 35, 38–39
third-order simulacra 55
Thrift, Nigel 59
Toda Poesia (All poetry; Leminski) 65
Toda Terça (Every Thursday; Saavedra) 51
Torto Arado (Crooked plow; Junior) 116
trace 74

traumatic realism 29–30, 50–51
traumatophilia 6–8

Untimely Meditations (Nietzsche) 4
urban realism 4, 27

Vattimo, Gianni 103
Verão Tardio (Late summer; Ruffato) 116–17
violence 26, 50–51
vista particular, A (Lísias) 75
Viva o povo brasileiro (Ribeiro) 11

Wallerstein, Immanuel 88
Warhol, Andy 30, 50
Watt, Ian 26
Weizman, Eyal 16
Weltliteratur (world literature) 87–99
Western realism 46
What Am I Doing Here 79
Woolf, Virginia 46
wound culture 14, 51

Žižek, Slavoj 15, 98

www.ingramcontent.com/pod-product-compliance
Lightning Source LLC
Chambersburg PA
CBHW021833300426
44114CB00009BA/421